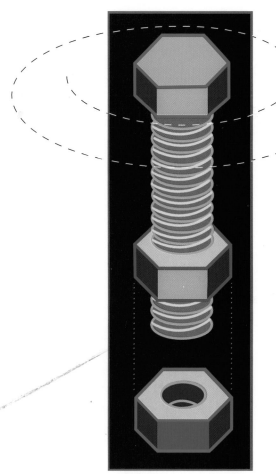

ISBN 0-942604-48-2

Library of Congress Catalog Card Number
(95-080875)

DISTRIBUTORS TO THE TRADE IN THE
UNITED STATES AND CANADA:

F&W Publications, Inc.
1507 Dana Avenue
Cincinnati, Ohio 45207

DISTRIBUTED THROUGHOUT THE
REST OF THE WORLD BY:

Hearst Books International
1350 Avenue of the Americas
New York, New York 10019

PUBLISHED BY:

Madison Square Press
10 East 23rd Street
New York, New York 10010
Phone (212) 505-0950, Fax (212) 979-2207

INNOVATIVE LOW BUDGET DESIGN
IS A PROJECT OF :

Supon Design Group, Inc.
International Book Division
1700 K Street, NW
Suite 400
Washington, DC 20006

Printed in Hong Kong

INNOVATIVE
LOW BUDGET
DESIGN

TODAY MORE THAN EVER, WE MUST STRETCH
THE DESIGN DOLLAR, BE CREATIVE, AND GET
DOWN TO THE NUTS AND BOLTS OF DESIGN

[SUPON DESIGN GROUP]

PROJECT DIRECTOR & CREATIVE DIRECTOR:
Supon Phornirunlit

JACKET DESIGNER:
Andrew Dolan

BOOK DESIGNER:
Richard Law

WRITER:
Linda Klinger

EDITOR:
Wayne Kurie

DESIGN EDITORS:
Jacques Coughlin, Andrew Dolan, Maria Sese Paul,
Supon Phornirunlit, Sharisse Steber

ASSOCIATE BOOK DESIGNERS:
Kimery Davis, Mimi Eanes, Deborah N. Savitt,
Lee Shaffer, Khoi Vinh

CAMERA SERVICES:
CompuPrint, Washington, D.C.; Color Imaging Center,
Washington, D.C.; The Photo Link, Washington, D.C.

PHOTOGRAPHERS:
Oi Veerasarn, Debbie Accame

*We acknowledge Gerald McConnell of Madison Square Press,
without whose assistance this book would not have been possible.*

T A B L E
— OF —
CONTENTS

INTRODUCTION

Designing on a budget?
Enjoy the challenge!

Contrary to what you may think, the lower the budget, the greater the opportunity for designers to shine. Now's the perfect time to experiment—develop that idea long shelved. Try something outrageous and extraordinary. Have fun—maybe even revive the potential of design simplicity with watercolors, string, cardboard, or crayons.

The key to successful, innovative low-budget solutions is self-confidence. Rest assured that the budget challenge does not bode well with less experienced designers, or those insecure with where their skills can take them. Small budgets don't mean the jobs will require less work—more often than not, the opposite holds true. One must start with a great concept, not a half-hearted one, and push it to its limits; infuse it with a lot of thought and not much money. Designers who are most successful with this approach are those who can draw on their knowledge of the craft and build on an original idea economically, without overseasoning it with extraneous flairs.

As with writing, brevity counts—especially when you're counting every penny. In the 400-page novel, there's plenty of time to bolster a weak sentence or develop an unfocused idea. In a short story, however, every line is critical, with no room to distract the reader from poor word choice. When design budgets are tight, each element works harder to deliver the message. The design probably won't have the luxury of expensive techniques to share the communication burden. Here is where you must strip off the excess weight—the baubles that please the eye but contribute little else—and ensure the elements used don't collectively push the total fee over that bottom line. Low-budget solutions excel by reducing the project to its nuts and bolts.

The challenge in great low-budget design is technique as well as thought, and you'll find plenty of inspiring ideas in this book. The low-budget approach may be, for example, the use of unique tools, such as rubber stamps to imprint a graphic. Or it could be adhering pressure-sensitive labels to a package as a design element. Costs can be kept low and impact high by experimenting with printing processes, such as the application of opaque inks. The format of the piece, its size or shape, can be altered, stretched, or shrunk with impressive—and inexpensive—results. Designers can try various methods of assembly to put a piece together in an interesting way—with brads, rings, or stacked like cards in a deck—without much added cost. One excellent way to add originality and vitality to a design is by incorporating copy that's high on perspective and verbal wit. A wide range of inexpensive but attractive papers, recycled or not, can also contribute to reducing the project's bottom line.

Of course, there are plenty of designs that simply look better with limited colors or flourishes, and have become low budget by accident, simply because that approach works so well. Regardless of whether they have the money for a more expensive design, many clients are reconsidering spending it when low-budget solutions can provide such ingenuity.

In *Innovative Low Budget Design*, you'll find a broad cross-section of work culled from almost 2,000 entries we received from 26 countries, from India and Portugal, to Russia and Canada. With such an array of both compelling and playful works, producing this book once again demonstrated the unlimited number of ideas that can be applied to design. We were so impressed with some concepts, you'll find them featured as our Innovative Design Excellence Awards (IDEA). We also devoted a section, "Maximize Your Creativity," to focusing on a collection of impressive, low-cost design techniques.

We've produced enough graphic design books to recognize patterns that emerge in this type of design competition, but the entries to *Innovative Low Budget Design* surprised even us. Project inclusion in past books has averaged from five to seven percent of the total entries; this time, we skimmed an incredible 12% off the top to include here—resulting in one of the largest design collections we have ever published, approaching 250 pro bono, limited color, or limited budget projects. Of those, submissions were classified into 15 categories: packaging; label or tag; shopping bag; stationery or identity; newsletter; brochure; annual report; catalog; book; poster; signage or billboard; point-of-purchase display; self-promotion; announcement or invitation; and miscellaneous. Judging criteria included:

- Clarity of concept
- Originality
- Applicability to target audience
- Effectiveness of strategy
- Design
- Adherence to a low budget

As always, certain commonalities are evident when you review such a huge amount of design. Recycled was by far the preferred paper, and paper color was widely used as an integral part of the designs. Supporting elements ranged from coy and whimsical (bows, ribbons, and twigs) to witty (rope, keyrings, and industrial components). You reminded us that exhibits are not simply square signage or billboards anymore. We saw many examples of hand assembly and hand-drawn invitations and announcements. And, as always in these competitions, we also saw a fair percentage of impractical pieces. It's a philosophy we share with much of the design community that when we choose design to exhibit in our books, it must not only be creative, but also equitably serve its business function.

Blueprints debuted as an excellent and practical design concept (page 23). Nicholas Associates got a special nod of approval because theirs was not only a stand-out solution, but fit the project so well—an annual report for a foundation managing the restoration and preservation of a temple. Jimmy Bonasoro and Kirk Miller's sandpaper moving announcement exhibited a fresh concept for an ordinarily proletarian endeavor (page 162). And we couldn't fail to highlight Tadeusz Piechura's poster (page 17), which displayed not only an ingenious use of hand-die-cutting and paper placement (only two silkscreened pieces were used), but also portrayed the project's arcane "jazz" atmosphere in a compelling way. Then there were the pieces that delivered the message and were, simply, fun, like Kleiner + Bold's delightful flip book (page 18), The Letterbox's booklet series *Qwerty* (we highlighted Issue 5 on page 96), celebrating Australian typographic issues, and Kirk Miller's moving announcement (page 7) that not only *moved*, but posed, strode, and ran.

Designers are discovering that the circumstances that dictate low-budget solutions are becoming more common, providing more opportunities to stretch the design dollar. Like eco-friendly design, graphic pieces with a lower price tag are often looked upon favorably by the public for their secondary message of modestness and restraint. Certain organizations, especially non-profits, find that lower-priced designs not only meet with their mission statements, but they also add a positive political stance to their posture in the industry. Opportunities for pro bono work always abound and will continue to do so; design studios can help out a favorite school, charity, church, or cause, and reap promotional benefits as well from the added exposure. Keep in mind that "low budget" is a relative term and doesn't always mean inexpensive—sometimes a "lower" budget can be achieved for a project that historically costs hundreds of thousands of dollars. Possibly the most common circumstance, however, is the client with limited funds to spend. But all of these scenarios offer more chances to develop a new direction to answer a client need.

We thank you, our readers and contest participants, for giving us the opportunity to review a selection of some of the most outstanding low-budget design in the world. This experience has served to underscore the fact that unique materials and a great idea together will only take design so far—more important is that the work fits the client and its objectives. Design, after all, must have coherence to be effective, and must please the client. We think this book contains some of the most meaningful and professional works we've seen.

We look forward to seeing more new work from our readers who have not yet submitted graphics to us for publication. In the meantime, we hope this book will leave you happily anticipating that upcoming project—and its budget constraints. Roll up your sleeves and have lunch delivered—here's a chance to show off what you do best!

Supon Phornirunlit is principal of Supon Design Group, where he also serves as creative director. Since founding the studio in 1988, he and his design team have earned more than 600 industry awards, including recognition from every major national design competition. Supon serves on the boards of directors of the Art Director's Club of Metropolitan Washington and the Broadcast Designers' Association, and is a frequent speaker at various industry organizations and universities. The studio's work has been featured in such recognized publications as Graphis, Communication Arts, Print, Step-by-Step, Studio, *and* HOW Magazine.

M A X I M I Z E
Y O U R
C R E A T I V I T Y

Low-budget design projects provide a great excuse to dig out the clay, colored pencils, scissors, and construction paper and simply *play* with shapes, materials, and details. You don't need special techniques to develop these ideas—just cleverness and persistence, qualities innate to most designers anyway. The following solutions demonstrated commercial as well as aesthetic innovation, once again proving that money isn't everything, especially when you've got a great design mind in your corner.

Who says two-color design always has to be the *same* two colors? Here, Communication Arts Co. and Denis Schwarz have the benefit of low two-color expense, but with one color providing the consistent design element, the other color can represent every rainbow hue. Several examples viewed side by side display a technicolor bouquet (far left). And no need to restrict this concept to colors—vary images, like Rauscher Design did, for a new look with every mailing (left).

Flat postcards and paper are effective, but they won't puff out a pillow. Deliver two postcards with appropriate die or hand-cuts, though, and you've got the beginnings of dimension. The recipient can assemble the design and pose it on a desk. CMF&Z Design (bottom) and the Leonhardt Group (right) used the concept to get attention and involve the recipient in the process, so s/he is less likely to quickly discard it.

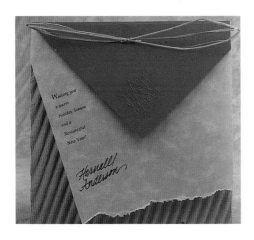

How different can you be? As different as these pieces—which are totally original but still deliver their commercial message. The solution from Hornall Anderson Design Works (above left) sports corrugated board, tissue, red paper, and gold braid in a magnificent collage, wrapped and mailed in an envelope. Also featured is Wöhlnick Design's wedding invitation of balsa wood, knotted gold cord, and recycled cardboard (above middle). And don't confine CD box packages simply to compact discs—package your promotion inside, like Kirk Miller and John Klein did (above right).

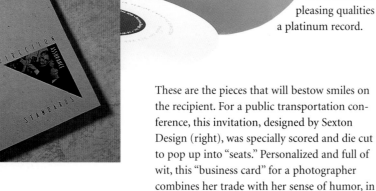

Books, brochures, and promotions don't have to be square or rectangular—circular, triangular (*à la* John Kirk), or even cut to assume animal shapes are effective approaches. One studio capitalized on its name—Platinum Design— by creating a promotion-in-the-round, and implying crowd-pleasing qualities similar to that of a platinum record.

These are the pieces that will bestow smiles on the recipient. For a public transportation conference, this invitation, designed by Sexton Design (right), was specially scored and die cut to pop up into "seats." Personalized and full of wit, this "business card" for a photographer combines her trade with her sense of humor, in a design from Pea Pod Studio (bottom).

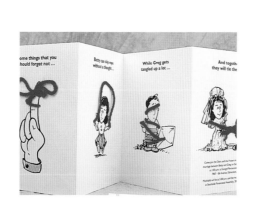

Incorporate "things" in your design for interest and entertainment. Firehouse Graphics, John Brady Design Consultants, and GKV Design discovered rope, string, and twigs are easy to find and long on creative value (above). Or try making a catalog like this one, from Weaver Design, with a cover of chipboard, cover copy printed on an white adhesive label, details added with rubber stamps, then bound together using grommets (left). Not much printing, but the assembly alone catches the eye. Metal is another outlet in this promotion, Sharisse Steber's compilation of things expected, and not (right).

Often, one can avoid expensive production techniques by substituting less expensive ones. Rubber stamps can sometimes replace offset printing and hand-cutting, for small quantities at least, may make high-cost die-cuts unnecessary. Wingrove & Wingrove Design Studio and Communication Arts Co. did, with outstanding results (right). Or imprint a design by outputting it directly from the computer onto color transparencies, and sandwich them between two die-cut paper TV frames. Then use pipe cleaners for antennas, the way the designers did at WLVI-TV (bottom).

Designers can't miss with posters—they're hard to ignore and big on impact. Atelier Tadeusz Piechura got the effect of a bizarre die-cut without the expense by taping two pieces of poster-sized paper together (on the reverse side) to simulate torn paper. An added benefit is its oversized result (top). And, speaking of oversized, here's Big Design Group's king-sized (almost six feet tall) blueprint clearly announcing its event in detail, without any offset printing at all (right).

Lowering the Cost Without Lowering the Standards

Looking for a good starting point for great design results without added expense? Here are some tips we've collected from a few of the design firms featured in this book, as well as some of our own:

- Think "alternative": For interest, use folds instead of die-cuts. For drama, use type and color instead of embossing or laminating. Use staples and tape instead of binding. If the solution has something to attach, do it yourself (or talk your neighbors, roommates, or kids into it). Clip art is more lively and interesting than ever before. Alter the normal approach and retrofit the project.

- Use what's already available—or scrounge: Use the laser printer or color copier to "print" brochures or newsletters. Use your friendly printer's leftover paper as the basis for your new design. If you don't have enough of one style of paper to complete your project, use different types of "found" paper for each piece—

or mix papers within a piece. Use up those envelopes with your old return address (before you moved) by coming up with a creative way to conceal the address, or use it as a design element. Construction or kraft paper can make excellent components to all sorts of designs.

- Launch an ordinary object in a new direction: Shape is a sure attention-getter (as in the brochure from the Office of Mayer & Myers Design, page 73, and John Kirk's triangular annual report, page 22). One of our favorite pieces in *Innovative Low Budget Design* is the photographer's transparency used as a business card—if the thicker "card" doesn't get your attention, the photo will (page 58).

- Don't rush great design: A compelling concept can be ruined with lack of appropriate execution.

- Use design to economically deliver two messages at once: A project that obviously has saved money can promote a positive work

ethic as well as its more obvious commercial objective. This is especially effective for those repositiories for financial data—annual reports.

- Look for a foundation on which to build: Designs based on themes can work well. For time-sensitive pieces, use holidays (don't forget the less popular ones, like Halloween or St. Patrick's Day). For themes with longevity, use humor, or focus on client mission statements that won't soon expire. For example, a firm whose principal advocates environmental awareness can deliver a side message via his/her design project through the use of found objects—low budget, and it also recycles.

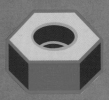

INNOVATIVE DESIGN EXCELLENCE AWARDS

INVENTING, SAID AMERICAN ENGINEER CHARLES F. KETTERING, IS A COMBINATION OF BRAINS AND MATERIALS; THE MORE BRAINS YOU USE, THE LESS MATERIALS YOU'LL NEED. THE DESIGN PROJECTS INCLUDED IN THIS SECTION DESERVE SPECIAL HONORS FOR THEIR USE OF MODERATION MIXED WITH INTELLIGENCE TO PRODUCE INVENTIVE WORKS GUARANTEED TO EXHILARATE THE CREATIVE MINDS IN US ALL.

Project:
Edana Reps Stationery

Design Firm:
Visual Dialogue

Art Director:
Fritz Klaetke

Designer:
Fritz Klaetke

Typographer:
Frank Klaetke

Client:
Edana Spicker

"We wanted a functional, rough-and-ready, hardworking look," says Fritz Klaetke when asked to describe this stationery design in one sentence. His client is an artists' representative—photographers, illustrators, and multimedia specialists—but she wasn't interested in a look with baubles and frills. Beyond the budget, which was limited, the designer's main consideration was to create something that showed the client's straightforward approach. "Her competition all had slick identifiers," said Fritz. "She wanted to avoid that overdesigned look." The audience for the stationery would be mostly art directors and designers, so he needed to incorporate professionalism and a bit of artistry. "The use of stickers allowed for an adaptable approach," Fritz notes.

Three of the components—the business card/sticker, envelope closure, and mailing label—were printed on a single sheet of label stock and pinhole perforated. Single elements could be torn out as needed and used for applications that would range from customizing existing material (elements could be applied to a reprint from an ad book or samples from magazines), to functioning with "found" stationery elements (for example, applied to chipboard).

Fritz gave the piece a little extra personality by having his father—an architect—do the type. "He had an old typewriter in his office, and I needed some old type," Fritz laughed. "So he typed what I needed, and I scanned it in."

Project:
Rod Bowkett Self-Promotional CD

Design Firm:
Pentagram

Art Director:
Justus Oehler

Designer:
Justus Oehler

Illustrator:
Justus Oehler

Client:
Rod Bowkett

The client, a freelance composer, wished to distribute his self-promotional CD, featuring 41 of his own compositions, to prospective clients. He wanted the package design to be competent, elegant, and to display a lot of character. But because so many of the CDs would be giveaways, the composer asked that production costs be as low as possible.

Despite the minimal budget for production, the designer, Justus Oehler, knew he could create a CD cover unique enough that it would stand out from its competition and be (hopefully) unforgettable. The solution evolved into a predominantly white CD cover ("almost luxuriously plain," remarked Justus) with an illustration in its center—a face made of musical notes, looking straight at you. "I chose this illustration," Justus explained, "because it gave the cover the intense personality it required." The designer chose the lowest possible specification costs for the cover. It took a little time, however, for the composer to accept that *less* would be *more.* "It was not easy to convince the client to go for this minimal color design, when the same spec would have allowed for a full-bleed color picture!"

A row of numerals at the right-hand side indicates the number of pieces on the CD. It had appeared on a print-out by accident, "but it looked good," said Justus, "so I decided to leave it there." The final design fully expresses the intent that recipients would feel they were given something rare and special. "It is the luxury of 'wasted space,' however, which makes this CD look precious."

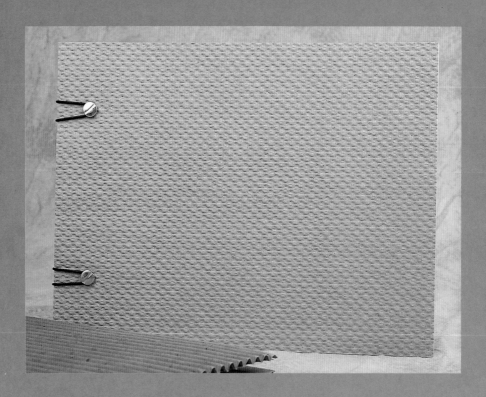

Project:
Rauscher Design Inc. Information
Packet

Design Firm:
Rauscher Design

Designers:
Russ Jackson, Janet Rauscher

Copywriter:
Russ Jackson

Client:
Rauscher Design Inc.

"We had been sending promotions typed on letterhead in a folder," said Janet Rauscher, an industrial designer by degree, "but the recognition factor from recipients was low. With some planning and without increasing our budget, we started producing this piece on the laser printer." And the response? "Incredible," says Janet. "Clients will always at least call when they receive it."

With their mailing limited to only about 20 every other month, the studio personalizes the promotion for each recipient. They use handmade paper ("the type you buy one sheet at a time"), and have it trimmed for free. A visit to the local electrical supply store yields O-rings, which they buy in bulk, and the Chicago screws and corrugated cardboard are left over from previous jobs. The cardboard is cut by their receptionist, and they scrounge leftover cover stock from printers. "The object was not to show our work, but to create interest in the company through its philosophies and accomplishments," Janet explained. And because no two are alike, they can raise the low-cost parameters slightly and use a higher quality paper when it is appropriate for the client. Their unusual approach delivers a promotion that's very striking, but not glitzy, underscoring the studio's style.

Project:
Faces of Hope Letterhead and
Raffle Tickets

Design Firm:
Y's Communication Pty Ltd

Creative Director:
Phil Young

Designer:
Simon Fuentes

Client:
Amnesty International–Australia

The letterhead and raffle tickets were donated to the client for its major fundraising event—the "Faces of Hope" mask auction. Over 100 prominent Australian and international artists and celebrities were invited to paint or treat a generic plastic mask while contemplating the theme, "Human Rights Transcend Gender and Culture." The end result was an astounding collection of work that represents a wide range and diversity of artistic interpretation. These print projects successfully exhibit the title and product of the event and carry the universal message underlying all human rights work undertaken by the client organization.

The images used were masks taken directly from the Amnesty International auction catalog, to which a duotone technique was applied to create a dramatic visual effect while remaining cost effective. The embracing warm orange hue, that contrasts with black for duotone versatility, communicated concepts of relationships, caring, and humanity. Saturating the midtones added a sepia tonality to the colors for a hazy, ethereal look. Typography was used to depict two forces: the strongly emphasized horizontal visuals describe movement in time as well as direction; the vertical, reinforced with the logo and arrow, indicate an upward direction and signify hope and future prosperity.

Project:
Postcards from the Global
Business Revolution Promotion

Design Firm:
Bielenberg Design

Art Director:
John Bielenberg

Designer:
John Bielenberg

Photographer:
Doug Menuez

Printer:
Lithographix

Client:
Gilbert Paper Company,
Mead Paper Company,
Doug Menuez

An intriguing title and translucent cover top this card collection, a giveaway at the Aspen Design Conference, which broadcasted the skills of three clients: two paper companies and a photojournalist. Because of the peer audience, including art directors and graphic artists, John Bielenberg felt somewhat pressured to produce something extraordinary. "It was a tough audience; in a sense, they'd seen everything already, and I was challenged to design something so interesting, they'd take notice," John said. "I wanted it to be witty, and to focus on the theme of the conference, which was about redefining business in the graphic community." Because the budget was so low, John was also restricted in some of the techniques he could use.

Initially, John wanted to pursue the idea of a tiny photo brochure. "Gilbert Paper suggested postcards," he said, "and that idea evolved into a postcard series," with its foundation in the photos. Photo selection came from the journalist's portfolio, and John interspersed appropriate quotes about business and change among the images. Since he felt that the longevity of the piece was an important consideration, John combined all the photos in a group secured by a silver ring that could be opened and refastened as postcards were removed and mailed.

His clients were pleased with the result, but John especially liked the concept of using limited ink and paper, and that there was an extended life for the communication after the initial message was delivered. He noted, "If the recipient spends some time with it, reads it and studies the photos, it communicates the clients' general point of view by making consistent statements about business and change through its photo choice."

Project:
We're on the Move
Announcement

Design Firm:
Kirk Miller

Art Director:
Kirk Miller

Designer:
Kirk Miller

Illustrator:
Supon Design Group

Client:
Kirk Miller

After moving his office seven times in three years, Kirk Miller had a good handle on the ins and outs of developing creative moving announcements.

"This one came to me quickly," Kirk said. "I conceptualized it in one evening, and was at the printer the next day, getting estimates." In fact, this was his first moving announcement that was actually completed before he moved. Classic in its simplicity, the design made use of components Kirk already had. The brads attaching the figure's limbs gave the piece a 3-D perspective, "and they were laying around the house anyway." He had purchased Supon Design Group's *Iconopolis* book (a collection of copyright-free icons for graphic use) for another project, and paged through it in search of a car. "I really wanted the piece to *move*," Kirk explained, "so I initially thought I'd put wheels on it."

Instead, what evolved was this piece, reminicent of a 1940s, vintage paper doll, which was folded to fit in a #10 envelope and sent to 250 recipients. Colors were chosen for their industrial, somewhat aged quality. The logo on the suitcase was similar to a contractor's mark one sometimes sees on sidewalks, and influenced his current logo.

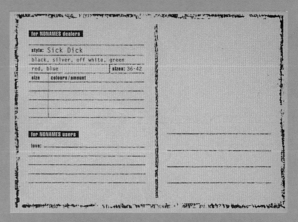

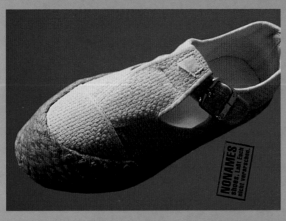

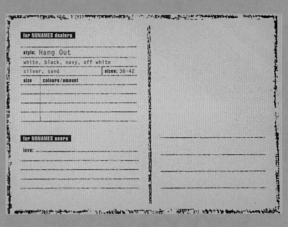

Project:
Nonames Shoes Catalog

Design Firm:
Baxmann & Harnickell Agentur
für Design GmbH

Art Director:
Felix Harnickell

Designer:
Kerstin Weidemeyer

Photographers:
Ralph Mecke (people),
Stefan Forsterling (shoes)

Client:
Nonames GmbH, Pirmasens

Nonames, a new brand in the shoe industry, specializes in unusual styles for teenagers, age 14 to 17. The client further divided its market into several groups, including Rappers, Techno/Ravers, Punks, and Slackers, who are nonetheless united in their rejection of The Establishment. Nonames is their anti–brand, reflecting their attitude.

The designers recommended that the shoe manufacturer make the Nonames brand into a separate company, and its resulting mission statement evolved into the motto, "Don't be taken for a sucker." The new company's advisory board includes two 16-year-olds (elections are held annually) responsible for ensuring that Nonames is always made by the young generation, for the young generation. Because Nonames' founding principle states that an anti-brand cannot be supported by traditional advertising, communication is accomplished via shoe stores, events, and promotions directed solely at the target group.

As one would expect, Nonames' catalog is also unconventional, designed with the same blunt, direct attitude. There are no glossy pages here; instead, a group of postcards appropriately tied together with a shoestring display the new styles from a particular collection. Store managers place orders by completing forms on the back side of each postcard and mailing it in. Additionally, image postcards are also used as a Nonames promotion. They are given away to young consumers, who retain or collect them because of their provocative sayings, most of which cannot be translated into English, as they involve word plays only meaningful in German.

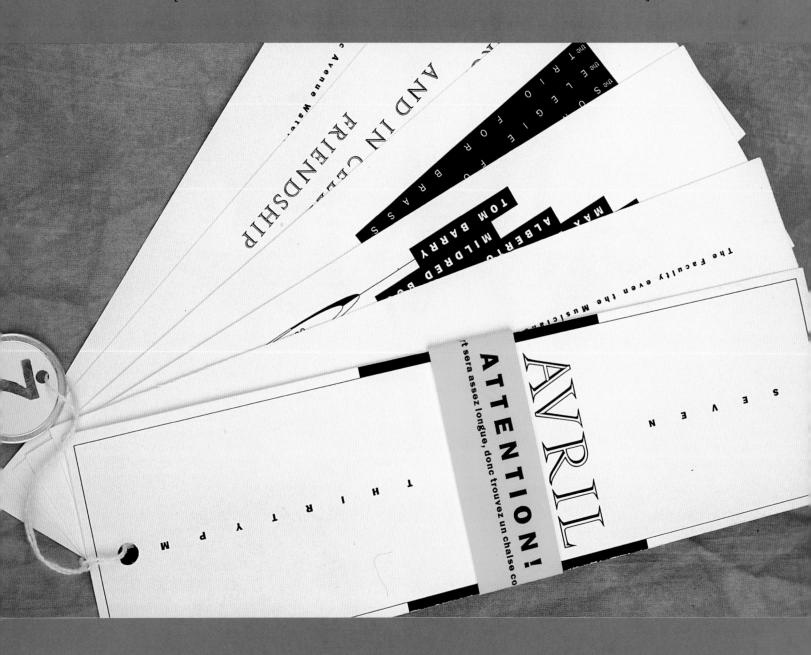

Project:
House Concert Invitation

Design Firm:
Philip Fass

Art Director:
Philip Fass

Designer:
Philip Fass

Client:
Harvey Hess

For this, the seventh in a series of invitations for chamber concerts produced by a local critic, Philip Fass wanted to cut through "the daily clutter of visual *detritus*" and reflect the quality of the music performed. Each invitation would be an "event" in its own right, with the piece setting the tone for the concert, to which select members of the art and civic communities had been invited. Production costs, however, could not exceed $150.

Phil used a key label to both disrupt the visual field around the invitation and act as a binding. "The idea of a series of cards was engaging," he said, "as each card could be different." Since the invitation was straight black-and-white, the typography had to be strong enough to carry the reader from card to card. A sense of music is embedded in the design and was intended to heighten anticipation of the event. And because the binding, a flourescent orange wrapper, provides a bright note of color and gives the invitation a toy-like nature, it engaged the reader in a way most visual material does not, inviting recipients, who are often busy, to stop and get the necessary information in a playful way. The format worked especially well because it did not prevent access to the information.

The print run was only 200 pieces, so originals were output on a laser printer on a 8.5" X 11" sheet. The pieces were trimmed and hand assembled, then mailed or hand delivered. Translated, the invitation reads, "Attention! Arrive early and find a comfortable chair."

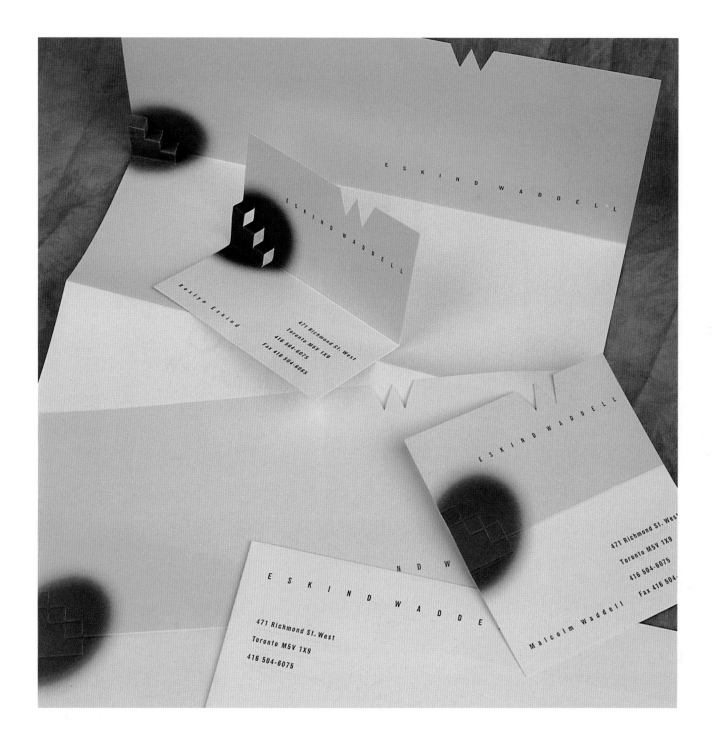

Project:
E.W. Stationery

Design Firm:
Eskind Waddell

Art Directors:
Malcolm Waddell, Roslyn Eskind

Designer:
Nicola Lyon

Printer:
Grafo

Client:
Eskind Waddell

Because the company had moved locations, it "gave us the opportunity to rethink the stationery," notes designer Nicola Lyon, adding that the studio was looking for a stylish, modern approach. The only things they couldn't change, however, were the die-cuts. So they reused the original dies (a bonus for budget-conscious designs) and introduced new stock and a type application with bolder colors. The result was an inspired look, low-budget but fresh and more contemporary—without breaking entirely with the studio's original and characteristic design concept.

The stationery hadn't been changed in years, and the designers started out by trying to include numerous elements in the design. But by the end of the project, they had streamlined it to an uncomplicated, straightforward typographic application, which allowed the dominant "E" and "W" elements to prevail. Originally, the designers also wanted to print up to the edge of the die-cut "E," but foresaw problems that could arise due to registration between the ink and the edge of the slits. The ellipse, which overprints the green background and is also integrated into the cream-colored stock, was an attractive solution. So as to avoid changing the tone of blue, they printed the green behind the vignette, adding an interesting, slightly hazy effect.

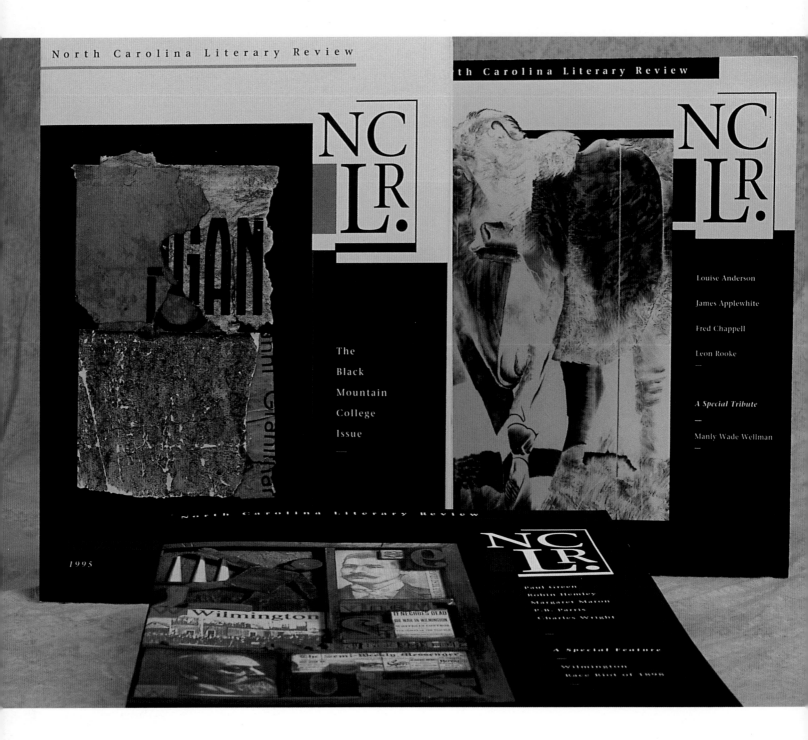

Project:
N.C. Literary Review, Vol. I, No. 2;
Vol. II, No. 1; Vol. II, No. 2

Design Firm:
East Carolina University School of Art

Art Directors & Designers:
Eva Roberts, Stanton Blakeslee

Editor:
Alex Albright

Cover Illustrators:
Catherine C.E. Walker (Vol I, No. 2);
Ray Elmore (Vol. II, No. 1);
Irwin Kremen (Vol. II, No. 2)

Cover Photographer:
Philip A. Burzynski (Vol. II, No. 1)

Client:
English Department, East Carolina
University

Published at East Carolina University, the staff that creates these magazines is a mix of faculty and students, all with a willingness to spend extraordinary amounts of time to produce publications of insight and significance. For many reasons, the publications have been described as combining "aspects of traditional academic journals with contemporary magazine design," but especially because of their consistently surprising, atypical placement of text on the page. This, emphasizes art director Eva Roberts, is text that is meant to be read. Although they strive to maintain readability, "we use a very flexible framework on which to structure the pages—no rigid formula, just enough format to provide a sense of unity for 228 pages." Rather than treating the typography in a straightforward manner, they instead build a distinctive context for individual articles, creating a rich—and diverse—visual experience that links editorial concept and design, and provides a forum for serious readers.

"The design process is one of evolution, working with pages on the computer screen," says Eva. "As each article makes a distinctive contribution to the whole, it is important to convey that meaningfulness when producing pages." An ongoing challenge is the lean budget; production funds, which come from donors and grants, are mostly spent on printing. For imagery, extensive—and creative—use is made of archival materials, which are readily available for a small charge, Eva says, "if one devotes time to researching the sources."

1994 POETRY SLAMs

National Championships

by Gene Hyde

BLACK, WHITE, and GRAY:

THE WILMINGTON RACE RIOT IN FACT AND LEGEND

by Bennett L. Steelman

By 8 o'clock on the morning of 10 November 1898, a crowd of about 500 armed white men had gathered at the armory of the Wilmington Light Infantry, on Market Street between Fourth Street and Fifth Avenue.

The Preacher

Sure they're dead. I don't know how or how come, or why, not having the divine intervention on the matter, but you can't tell me two snot-rag children are going to get out of this town without anyone seeing them. There's just the two ways of entering or leaving and that's by the one street going one way and the other going the other. So someone saw them.

Dust to dust and the Lord's will abideth! Hallelujah!

Knowing what I know about what goes on in this town, it can't abide soon enough. What I think? They are buried this minute in someone's backyard. Get in a backhoe, we'd find the bodies. I've preached till I'm blue in the face, but who listens? What's salvation to them only wants to lick ice cream of a Sunday? You can't stamp out the devil's work for he's like a mad dog once he gets going – or she – the scriptures don't discount she's a she, you know. Which is maybe why the devil's work is so cunning. It got baleful dark that morning, I know that. Like a twister's

s t r u c k .

Ask Minnie, my organist, she'll say the same.

Minnie, the Organist

I will not. I was at the organ. I didn't want to be, having a killer-cold. Don't need an organist anyhow. No one ever bothers to keep up. I've heard cows mooing in a meadow had more rhythm than that bunch. I saw nothing. Heard nothing. Well, this whine in my ears, these shivers – but that was my cold. Once, through the window, I see a white galloping horse. But it takes a lot in that church to make me turn around. I keep my back to that bunch and that's how I like it.

One time a man's pants caught fire, when Orson Johnson, the cross-eyed one, was playing with matches. I looked around then. That's the only time.

Orson

I'm the one she's talking about.

I strike a match and boom! – I'm a sheet of flames. The wife screeching and suddenly I'm bare-buttock naked in front of the whole congregation, because she's pulled down everything.

I saw the children go out. Saw this black creature at the door. I thought it was Death Death calling, and he was going to lay his hand over us all. End of the world, I thought. I tried to move but couldn't. My hair standing up on my head. "**Don't go, children! Run!**" The wife tells me that's what I was trying to say - but too scared to get it out. She's got her hand pinching my thigh, shooshing me.

Delilah Orson

"Shoosh, Orson, shoosh!" That's what I'm saying. He's gone pale. He's got sweat beads on his brow an inch deep. So I put my hand up over his man parts and I squeeze. "Stop it! Stay put!" I say. When I see this white horse galloping past the window, and this woman on it with streaming robe.

The children's mother, with this frantic face. She's crying, "Children, children! Run!" All in a blap of light. That's when I dig my nails into Orson's thing. Later on, we get the doctor in, he's got to have a tetanus shot. Infection lasts a month . . . And the children gone. Just gone. Their mother expiring the identical hour.

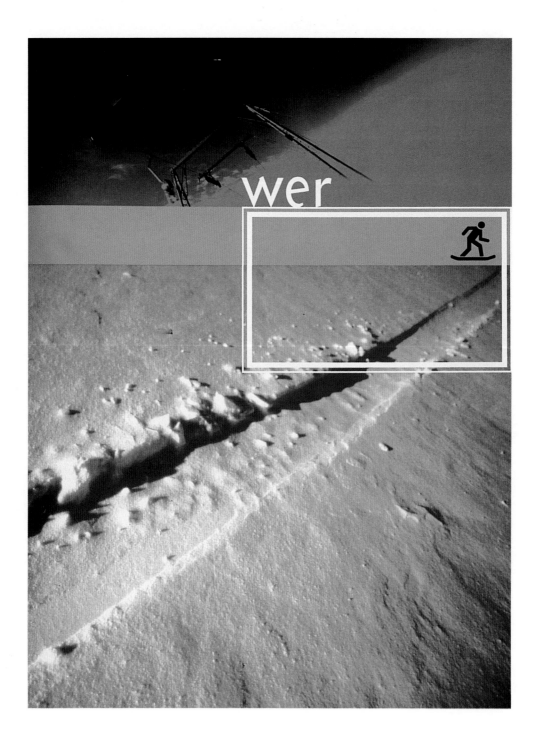

Project:
Wer—A Snowboard Analysis
Brochure/Magazine

Designer:
Olaf Becker

Illustrator:
Olaf Becker

Photographer:
Olaf Becker

Copywriter:
Olaf Becker

Client:
Diploma 1995-Graphic Design

Because the project addresses the new generation of individual action sports, especially snowboarding, *Wer* (i.e., who snowboards and why) is almost a sociological and analytical publication. Olaf Becker chose what he called "snowboard-specific colors" to give it a "non-colorful and calm face—brown for Earth and mountains, and blue for sky and snow." The sport itself, he says, has a lot of different "faces," so he designed the piece so that every page looked different and told a new story. To suggest the uniqueness of the design, the publication's title does not display a snowboarder.

The primary goal was to develop a visual and linguistic language to deliver the underlying message of snowboarding—a view apart from the commercial side, the sensation of being in the mountains. The graphic language had to be contemporary, informative, youthful, and address both snowboarders and non-snowboarders. Limited by a low budget, Olaf jumped at the chance when a friend offered to print the cover with five colors for free. That provided a little more money to spend on the interior paper and another two colors. He took all the photography himself, as pictures of lift wheels and snow tracks—the secondary components of snowboarding—were impossible to find.

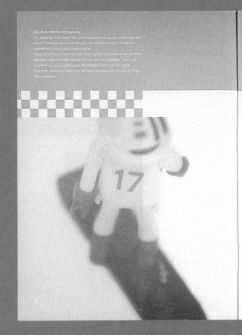

»It's about when you decided riding was your passion.

You needn't be a sidekick to him.

You can rip with the best of them.

It's the simple realization that

you have your own identity ...

We respect that.«

Wie es die anderen sehen

3.5

	Surfen*	Skateboarden	Skateboarden
Biken	Skateboarden	Surfen	Snakeboarden
Tennis	Biken	Skateboarden	Surfen
Skateboarden	Skifahren	Biken	Biken
Surfen	Inlineskaten	Snakeboarden	
Basketball	Wasserski	Inlineskaten	
Fußball	Fitness	Preise feilschen	
Schwimmen			
	Paragliden		
	? 36%	? 50%	? 18%	? 0%

ZUM SNOWBOARDEN GEHOEREN

SCHRAUBENZIEHER
VIDEOKAMERA
HOLZFAELLERHEMD
HEISSE DUSCHE
WODKA FEIGE
HALFPIPE
WEIZEN GAMEBOY
DOSENBIER
MUSIK AUF DER HINFAHRT
VW BUS
TIMBERLANDS
MARY JANE
SPRENGWAGEN
DROGEN SCHLEPPLIFTE
SCHAUFELN
ALPENDOLLAR
BLAUER HIMMEL BECKS
ISABEL
BLAUE FLECKEN

Project:
Transparent Color Studio
Letterhead and Identity

Design Firm:
Hon Design

Art Director:
Claudia Hon

Designer:
Claudia Hon

Client:
Transparent Color Studio

To create a unique letterhead and identity for a photography studio, Claudia Hon first had to consider the fact that there was no budget for printing. Not a problem, when you have a laser printer at your disposal— "black toner served as the printing press," she said.

The client name, Transparent Color Studio, immediately evoked the image of a transparency. Claudia started by designing the letterhead, drawing the shape of a transparency on paper. "I considered using the image as a logo," she recalls, "but then it occurred to me that the space inside the transparency could be used to frame the letter, so I enlarged the image." Next, she had to determine where to put the address information, and what font would be appropriate. After examining an actual transparency, she noticed that type runs up the left edge, so that's where the address went, using a font similar to what was on the real transparency. She rotated the entire image to give it more visual interest, and output it onto the laser printer. To make it look unique, she cut semi-transparent vellum sheets to size and, with her laser printer, gave them just the right effect.

The business card took the form of a 2.25" transparency printed on the same paper, but at that size, it curled and wasn't sturdy enough. After scouting around her studio, Claudia found a film sleeve cut a little larger than the card and put the card inside it—a perfect solution.

Vellum doesn't fold well into a regular-sized business envelope, so Claudia used a larger envelope so that the letter would only need to be folded in half. The final design greatly pleased the client in both form and cost— especially since letterhead, cards, and envelopes were produced for less than $50.

Project:
Jazz Grand Prix Melomani
'94 Poster

Design Firm:
Atelier Tadeusz Piechura

Art Director:
Tadeusz Piechura

Designer:
Tadeusz Piechura

Copywriter:
Ireneusz Kowalewski

Client:
Stowarzyszenie Jazzowe
"Melomani"

The Jazz Society "Melomani" of Lodz, Poland confers annual awards in jazz in three categories: Artist (Performer) of the Year (1994 Grand Prix Winner—Andrzej Jagodzinski); Reviewer/Journalist of the Year (Marcin Kydrynski); and Contribution to the World of Jazz (Music Academy in Katowicz—Jazz Department).

Tadeusz Piechura's already restricted budget was further reduced when one of his sponsors reconsidered financing this design project. Although Tadeusz was required to accomplish the design work on his own, the Jazz Society helped him by purchasing the gold, silver, and black papers. The Centrum Serigrafii Przy P.W.S.S.P. W Lodz (Silkscreen Center of Art College in Lodz) overprinted the black paper with white captions. Tadeusz cut the paper and arranged all three pieces into the final shape—an exquisite composition of color, line, and dimension that portrayed not only the honors bestowed on the award-winners, but the sophistication of the music in which they excelled.

The poster, which, said Tadeusz, "seemed very easy to carry out in my mind," turned out to be somewhat more expensive than he had anticipated—and impossible to produce at the Polish printing facilities accessible to him. "That is why," he explains, "there are only 50 copies available."

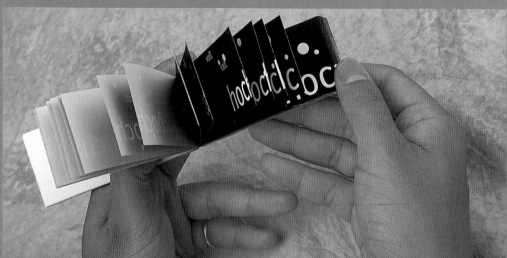

Project:
Drunter und Drüber
Self-Promotion

Design Firm:
Kleiner & Bold

Designers:
Tammo F. Bruns, Frank Schulte,
Karsten Unterberger

Client:
Kleiner & Bold

Some designs don't need deep analysis or multiple layers of imagery to be successful. Sometimes all they need is playfulness, like this piece from Kleiner & Bold. The incentive to create what the designers called a "flicker book" was a big summer party they had hosted for their new neighbors, with whom they had started a business partnership. The creation of this alliance was celebrated with clients and friends. The inspiration for the flip book, however, was the desire that guests who were invited but could not attend might nevertheless be able somehow to participate in the event. So the progress of the festivity was typographically condensed, "documented" by means of the flip book (where, when pages are flicked rapidly with the thumb, images flipping by seem as if they were animated), and mailed to appropriate invitees.

There is a double meaning to the phrase "*drunter and drüber*" (topsy-turvy), say the designers: the aspect of the physical location (the two firms occupy different floors in the same building—upstairs and downstairs); and the literal aspect (an accurate description of the party itself, was everything was turned upside-down). Produced by computer, the book required many dummies and trial-runs to achieve a harmonious and fluent motion of shapes and text. It was yet another odd but effective solution for this studio, which was established with neither a Mr. Kleiner nor a Mrs. Bold, but is managed instead by a Bruns, a Schulte, and an Unterberger.

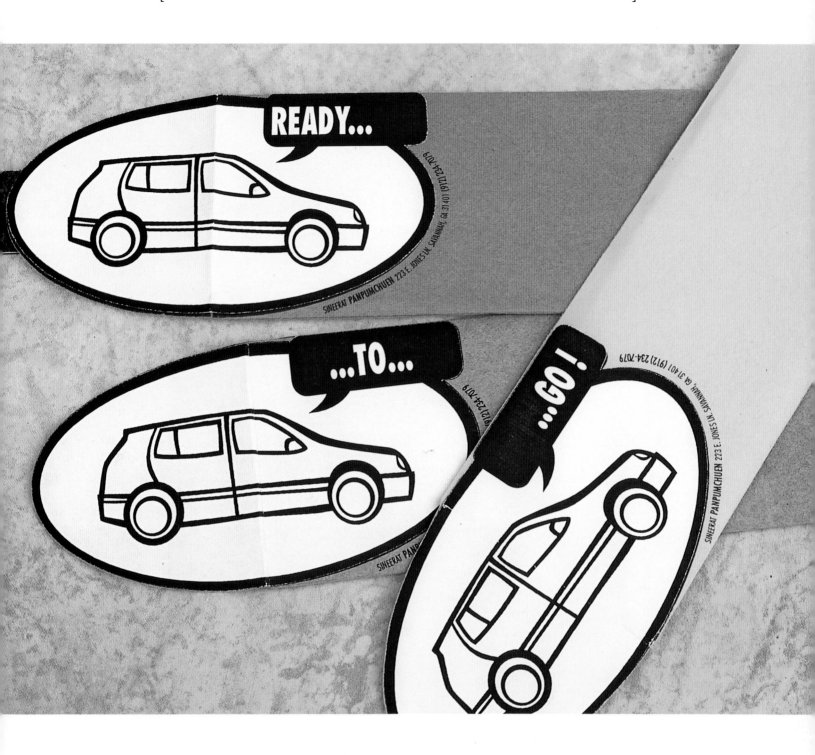

Project:
Ready To Go! Promotion

Designer:
Sineerat Panpumchuen

Illustrator:
Sineerat Panpumchuen

Client:
Sineerat Panpumchuen

A compact series of mailings, "Ready To Go!" was part of Sineerat Panpumchuen's self-promotion campaign as she neared college graduation, with her goal being an in-person interview. It was a very simple idea, easy to construct (the pull-tab slides out of a stiff paper "envelope" to reveal a variety of illustrations), and she hoped it would pique the interest of targeted design studios enough to contact her.

"The idea came to me because I would be moving on after graduation," explained Sineerat, so she sketched a map, car, and portfolio to illustrate her future plans. As it was a sequential group of pieces, she used three different colors for each mailing—blue, yellow, and red—primary colors aligned with the educational theme. The "Ready" piece is mailed first to target audiences; the remaining two pieces, "To" and "Go," then followed in order.

Low cost meant limiting the colors to two and keeping the piece lightweight and small enough to fit in a standard envelope, avoiding extra postage. Said Sineerat, "The construction paper brought back memories of my childhood art," and it was appropriate and inexpensive, as well. She found the paper's tactile qualities and subdued colors enhanced the image she tried to project. The tabs—which, when pulled, revealed puffs of "exhaust" from the cars—reinforced the concept of her journey into an exciting future.

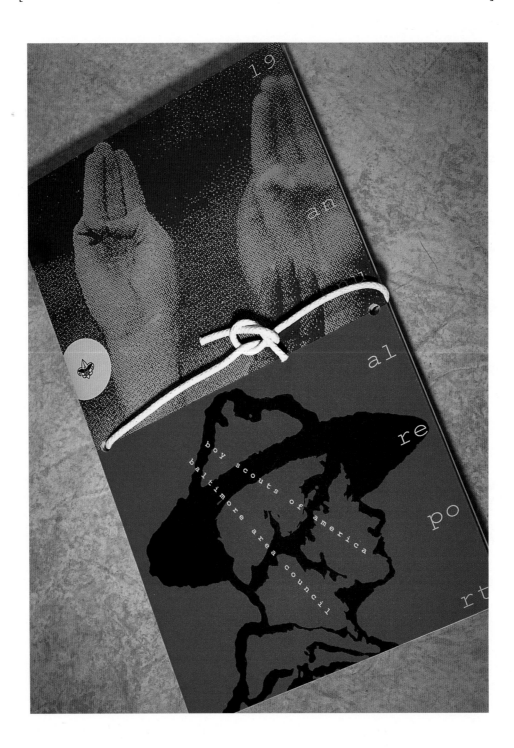

Project:
Boy Scouts of America
Annual Report

Design Firm:
GKV Design

Art Director:
Gene Valle

Designer:
Gene Valle

Photographer:
Boy Scouts of America Archives

Client:
Boy Scouts of America,
Baltimore Area Council

There are all sorts of ways designers can keep costs low. Gene Valle, with a ball of cord beside him one evening, tied almost 400 of these annual reports by hand while his cat looked on. The paper was donated, and existing photos were used, property of Scouting enthusiast Dr. Harris, who has archived "everything the Boy Scouts ever produced!" Gene claims. With such a supply at hand, Gene was able to include in the project some art that was so old, it was starting to disintegrate. It was one way of expressing the extraordinary history of Scouting.

This pro bono task had to function as both an annual report and a recruitment piece. With a focus on inner-city youth, it was fun to produce, and ensured the reader was involved via its interactive approach (you have to untie it to read it). "I tried to give it a spontaneous, workbook feel," Gene said. "Mostly, the design had to make sense—it was about youngsters and should reflect their interests." To avoid making it intimidating or authorative, and to keep it on the level of the youth it served, Gene, a former Scout himself, focused on depicting the positive aspects of membership. To provide that "affected" look, the piece included some handwork—inexpensive and well worth the result.

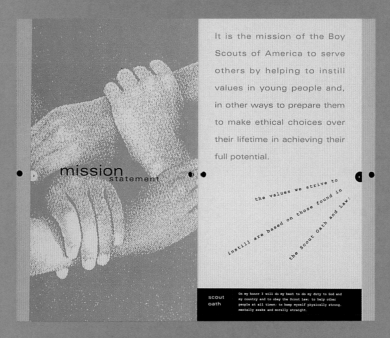

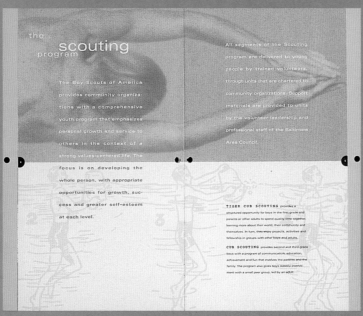

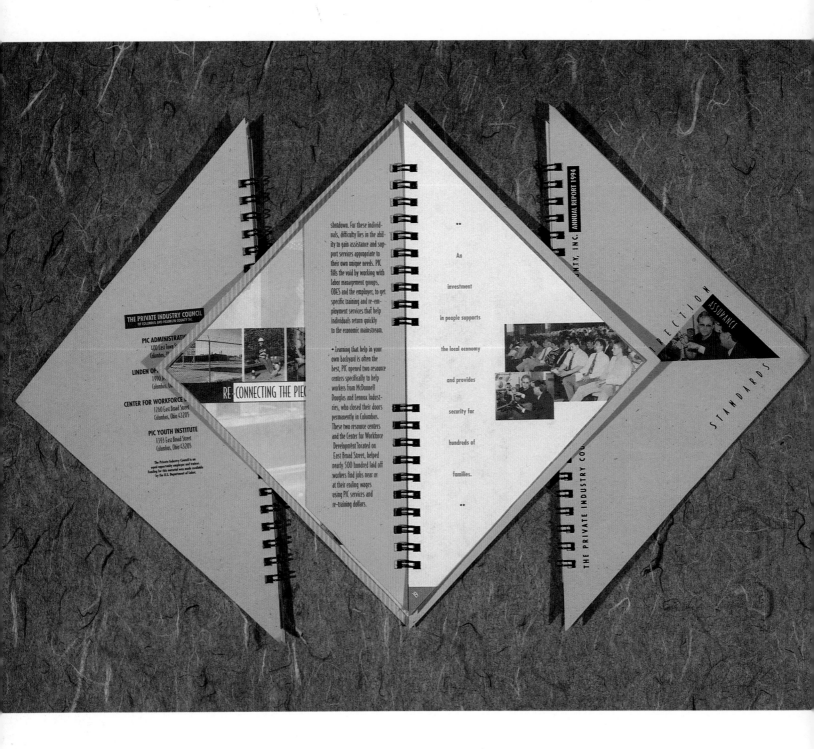

Project:
Private Industry Council
Annual Report

Design Firm:
John Kirk

Art Director:
John Kirk

Designer:
John Kirk

Photographer:
Linda Syguda

Printer:
Fine Line Graphics

Prepress:
Lithokraft II

Client:
The Private Industry Council
of Columbus and Franklin
County, Inc.

John Kirk was lucky—the client organization, a non-profit, publicly funded entity, was open-minded and progressive enough to let him try an unusual approach to annual report design, and it resulted in a piece that still fools recipients into thinking it costs thousands more than it did.

"I would like to say that I did 100 different sketches before developing the idea for the shape of this report, but I didn't," John admits. Instead, the client had presented him with a line drawing on a sheet of paper with the words "Direction," "Assurance," and "Standards" forming a triangular shape. "My immediate thought was that, instead of just making a triangular logo for the cover, why not make the entire book a triangle?" With the client's go-ahead, John set out to create a novelty that would break with the rigid protocol of the majority of annual report design. Open, the book forms a diamond shape, and these spreads were used primarily as the base on which to arrange the existing photos so that they worked together—the biggest design obstacle. In addition, vertical half-pages accent the text.

Price quotes for the printer to hand-cut the report were too high, so John used die-cuts to create this publication. The project remained surprisingly low budget, however, because he was able to negotiate inexpensive prices for the paper and printing. Selective use of different paper stocks makes the report appear to have been printed with more than just two color-compatible inks.

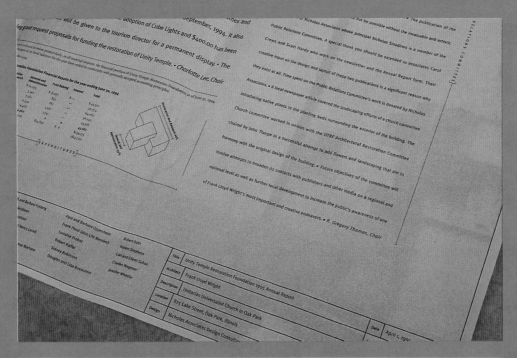

Project:
Unity Temple Restoration
Foundation Annual Report

Design Firm:
Nicholas Associates

Art Director:
Nicholas Sinadinos

Designers:
Nicholas Sinadinos, Scott Hardy

Illustrator:
Scott Hardy

Client:
Unity Temple Restoration
Foundation

A lightweight, oversized blueprint as an annual report? It's a concept that works incredibly well in this pro bono project, which exchanged traditional offset printing for a process typically the exclusive domain of the blueprinter (i.e., Diazo "blue" printing). Without press time, plates, or ink, this process saves money. One sheet at a time is printed from a film master, to which the designers output their file; contact-printing is the result.

Said Nicholas Sinadinos, "We do this project every year, and every year, the budget stays exactly the same," which means the fee actually decreases; so the designers are challenged by not only doing more with less, but also doing it differently than the last time. The poster was even folded using the recognized architectural method and sequence, and the envelope was stamped with return address information in the same manner in which an architect will stamp a drawing to identify it.

The overall design objective was to positively reflect the managing activities of the foundation, whose involvement includes overseeing restoration and preservation services for the temple. To create the impression of an architect's blueprint, they configured the typography to simulate various architectural shapes that comprise the temple, which was designed by architect Frank Lloyd Wright. One of the big challenges was to include an actual photographic image of the building in a very light value to read behind the overlaying copy (they experimented on the computer before going to press).

Project:
Bazaar Bizzoso
Arts Festival of Atlanta

Design Firm:
Lorenc Design

Art Director:
Jan Lorenc

Designers:
Jan Lorenc, Xenia Zed,
Dan Reynolds

Illustrators:
Jan Lorenc, Red Weldon

Photographer:
Rion Rizzo Creative Source
Photography

Collaborator:
Architectural Image
Manufacturers

Client:
The Arts Festival of Atlanta

This "bazaar" was actually an interactive worksite intended to break the tradition (and, some of the participants say, the monotony) of the Arts Festival in Atlanta. Environmental design criteria was to create a low-budget, environmentally friendly, recycled junk, funky, one-of-a-kind place. The final exhibit comprised 40,000 square feet and 40 artist stations designed to cause minimal stress to the park environment over the nine-day festival. One of the most effective ideas was the 40,000 hot pink, yellow, and blue utility marking flags, which formed concentric circles around the trees to protect their root systems by keeping people off. Participating artists were also asked to do something environmentally interactive and bizarre to their station/space, resulting in such endeavors as the "lizard booth" and the "Mr. Microphone" tent.

Sizes and scales were estimated, and no detailed drawings were done—only rough sketches. Everything was thrown together, the designers asserted, and built by "gut instinct." With a budget of only $500, virtually no money was spent unless it was donated. Project collaborators visited junkyards, convinced people to volunteer time and construction costs, and used anything and everything they could find to produce the outrageous event.

Lorenc Design designed the 20-foot tower of junk as the festival's focal point, with a series of signs to keep people off the grass, and a poem, written in honor of Gene Alcott, creator of the Bazaar Bizarre (later changed to Bazaar Bizzoso) and a well-respected Atlanta artist, who died just prior to its opening. The design made an incredible impact, although it rained for the entire nine days.

Project:
MWA Graphic Standards Manual

Design Firm:
CMF&Z Design

Art Director:
Brent Wirth

Designer:
Brent Wirth

Copywriter:
Mark Lunde

Client:
Metro Waste Authority (MWA)

This manual had to reflect the mission and culture of the client—environmentally friendly waste management—while establishing graphic standards for the client's new identity. CMF&Z Design developed this unique printed piece which allows for expansion (the binding can be taken off and new pages added without additional expense), and maintained a very limited budget.

"We felt the need to use recycled materials so that the manual would accurately reflect client values," explained Brent Wirth. The publication's utilitarian features were driven by this same philosophy of moderation and simplicity—the screw posts are a specific example of how the studio built versatility, flexibility, and a recycled "feel" into the piece. These unique posts, coupled with the unusual positioning of the binding at the top of the piece, reflect an unexpected approach. The use of a high recycled-content paper complemented this creative approach, and underscored the firm's intent to help the community by reducing waste. Finally, the use of "waste" images as texture help communicate a tactile feeling for the printed piece. Photos and Polaroids that illustrated areas of waste management, such as tires being used in landfill recycling, were selected from the an existing "library" of images taken by client employees.

Project:
Alfred Design Promotion

Design Firm:
Alfred Design

Art Director:
John Alfred

Designer:
John Alfred

Copywriter:
Carol Casey

Client:
Alfred Design

The biggest challenge in creating this promotion? Says John Alfred, "Determining an unconventional but effective method of binding." And, as an afterthought: , "Also, finding the printer to print it within budget." But the latter hurdle was conquered with old-fashioned hard work. To keep costs to a minimum, the printer delivered uncollated, trimmed, and folded pages. Collating and binding were done in the studio. To complete the piece, fasteners were hand-painted, holes drilled into the brochures by hand (with a cordless drill!), and each fastener slipped into place.

With the intent of creating an uncluttered showcase for the logo design capabilities of his studio, John began the design process with the selection of a diverse blend of logos. Two logos were then grouped together based on visual similarities and placed on pages opposite short descriptions of each. The brochure design conveyed a conservative yet contemporary image via its colors and choice of assembly. To underscore John's objective, introductory text states his definition of a successful logo—one that compresses complex messages into a concise visual thought, and marries thought and image into an immediately recognizable symbol.

MOLECULAR DYNAMICS COMBINES CORE
COMPETENCIES IN MOLECULAR AND
CELL BIOLOGY, LASER SCANNING, SIGNAL
PROCESSING, DETECTION TECHNOLOGIES
AND COMPUTER SCIENCE TO DEVELOP
INNOVATIVE IMAGING INSTRUMENTS
THAT INCREASE PRODUCTIVITY AND
ENABLE NEW ANALYTICAL TECHNIQUES
IN THE LIFE SCIENCE LABORATORY.

Project:
Molecular Dynamics
Annual Report

Design Firm:
Cahan & Associates

Art Director:
Bill Cahan

Designer:
Bob Dinetz

Photographer:
Holly Stewart

Client:
Molecular Dynamics

"The client wanted to cut the annual report budget in half, without losing the impact they had achieved the previous year," said Bill Cahan. Seeing that the last annual report was a huge promotional splash for the biotechnology firm, the designers knew they were in for a challenge.

But the studio specializes in annual reports, as well as packaging, and advertising, so they started by thinking in terms of minimal color, and then adapted a tabloid size for its novel, attention-getting effect. Because they couldn't afford to use photos, they made a large typographic treatment the design element. In addition, "the restrained pallette," said Bill, "reflected the client's new business strategy"—that is, no-nonsense, a somewhat "buttoned-up" tone. Actual graphics were simple and conveyed the leaner business approach. The designers focused on the business-to-business message emphasizing the client's technology and core competencies. "They were a great client to work for," Bill says, "as they were very open to our suggestions." The result pleased both client and designers.

"Annual reports are one of the most difficult things to design," Bill maintains. "You must understand the strategic business messages and, in this case, the technology involved. The client has a diverse audience, ranging from retailers to financial analysts, and the report is also used as a recruitment vehicle. We knew the CEO, however, just wanted someone to *read* it. The normal course of action is to do something safe; it's much harder to do something memorable. We think we took some risks and were successful."

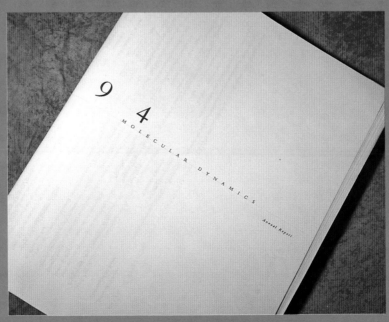

Project:
"Greek Life: Get A Feel For It"
Promotion

Design Firm:
Sayles Graphic Design

Art Director:
John Sayles

Designer:
John Sayles

Illustrator:
John Sayles

Client:
Drake University

Found objects and leftover materials can add interest to a project while keeping the budget in check. For this brochure—a fraternity/sorority "rush" recruitment mailing—designer John Sayles used paper remnants from a recently completed corporate project, scrap corrugated cardboard, and industrial/office supplies, such as warehouse shipping tags. The brochure comes packaged between two chipboard trays—the kind used to package meat in grocery stores—held together with shipping tape. Perhaps the most innovative material in the brochure is its front cover: an actual metal printing plate, ordinarily used for transferring ink to paper. Although never actually used in this printing process, the plate is burned with the project's theme, "Greek Life: Get A Feel For It," and embossed with the client's name, Drake University. Inside the brochure, the reader is treated to unexpected additions, such as adhesive labels (remnants of various university events), and two glassine envelopes, one containing a letter, the other, a 35mm slide of the campus.

This colorful collage approach was achieved with an eye towards economy. Paper pages were screenprinted with one color of ink (silver), while black ink was used on the chipboard. John describes the graphic approach he took with illustrations and typography as "rustic." "With the variety of materials used, it was important that the design be executed in the same 'un-slick' fashion," he added. "Some of the type was done on an ordinary typewriter, and the illustrations are certainly not what you'd call 'refined.'"

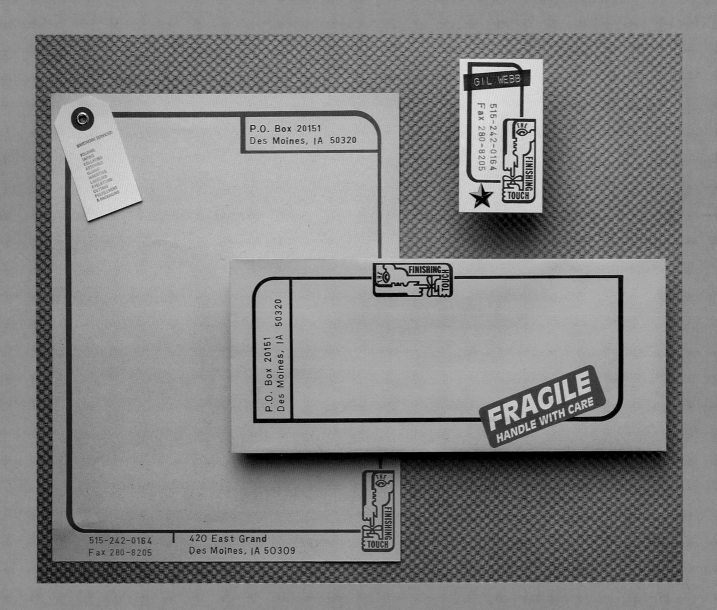

Project:
The Finishing Touch Letterhead

Design Firm:
Sayles Graphic Design

Art Director:
John Sayles

Designer:
John Sayles

Illustrator:
John Sayles

Client:
The Finishing Touch

A small Iowa bindery, The Finishing Touch provides finishing services to printers, including taping, labeling, eyeletting, and other handwork and fulfillment. Designer John Sayles wanted to develop a corporate identity for the firm that would reflect its custom niche. The resulting logo features a graphic character with its finger on a package bow. Individual components of the letterhead system are each printed on a different paper, with the envelopes a standard Kraft paper "policy" style, and the business cards printed on manila stock.

The true nature of The Finishing Touch project is condensed into the details of the letterhead program. The address on the envelope is hand-stamped in purple and a "Glass: Handle With Care" label provides an attention-getting feature. In addition to the printed logo and rubber-stamped information, the business card includes a hand-made plastic label with the employee's name, and a decorative plastic star hand-glued to each card. Similarly, the letterhead includes a miniature shipping tag (imprinted with a list of the company's services) applied with an eyelet.

Sayles explains the design process: "Because the client is a small company, they allowed me a lot of freedom to come up with a unique look. Their business is handwork, so they didn't balk when I came up with this rather involved process. The individual parts themselves are economical—actually, they're *cheap!*—and readily available. The client simply 'assembles' the components of their letterhead during their downtimes or as needed, so it works very well for them."

Project:
One Company Divided
Annual Report

Design Firm:
Vaughn Wedeen Creative

Art Director:
Steve Wedeen

Designer:
Steve Wedeen

Photographer:
Michael Barley

Computer Production:
Heather Scanlon

Printer:
Champagne Fine Printing

Paper:
Champion Benefit

Client:
Lasertechnics

It had been a significant year for the client firm, a small high-tech interest. They had determined that their two markets and product lines were so totally different, they could not be merged. So they literally split the company in half, with the Imaging division staying in Albuquerque, New Mexico, and the Marketing Division hiring a new CEO and moving to Dallas, Texas. The company wanted to express the positive aspect of the change—stock owners now owned shares in two companies with equivalent prospects for profitability. To communicate the approach of the senior CEO—a roll-up-your-sleeves, back-to-basics type of leader—the annual report would also avoid glossy photos or a slick presentation.

In the hands of Vaughn Wedeen, the report became a tangible, literal expression of the company and its message: the firm's division was reflected in a horizontally divided book (which included the qualifier "good news" to avoid the negative undertones "one company divided" may apply). Said Steve Wedeen, "We perforated the middle of the book, through the word 'company,' while it was being die-cut." The designers also split the colors.

The report was organized into four components. The opening text consisted of a letter from the senior CEO, detailing the company as a whole (one continuous letter, united from top to bottom). Reports from the CEOs of both companies comprised the second and third sections, which were treated as two separate blocks of text, one on the top of the divided book, one on the bottom. The last section was again united, as the finances were still represented by a single accounting system.

Project:
Kinos Aarau Logo and Stationery

Design Firm:
Wild & Frey

Art Director:
Heinz Wild

Designers:
Heinz Wild, Marietta Albinus

Client:
Kinos Aarau

To design a new logo and stationery for a small theater specializing in film noir, classics, and other select movies, the designers initially tried to translate the word "cinema" into a logo. Then they noticed that, because the number of letters in "Kinos" and "Aarau" were equal, they could typeset them instead into a black square to resemble a piece of film. Result: an extremely simple logo (one of the client's requests) which was also easy to apply in a variety of ways, with form and design reduced to the absolute minimum.

When designing the stationery, they played with the idea of hanging the logo off the top, as if it were a strip of film. This was easy to execute: they printed the black square, then die-cut the characters, cut off the unwanted paper, and folded the square downwards. Since the size of the logo was the same, they could use the same tool for die-cutting the business cards as well, and the envelope didn't need printing at all. A sticker, identical to the letterhead logo, not only identifies the movie theater but also functions as the address (there is only one "Aarau" in Switzerland, and Kinos Aarau is well known in the town, so no zip code or street identifiers are required). Light goes through the die-cut letters and casts silhouettes onto the paper—which was chosen for its functionality (it feeds easily through a laser printer).

Project:
Annual Report

Design Firm:
Wild & Frey

Art Director:
Heinz Wild

Designers:
Heinz Wild, Martha Eisschiel

Photographer:
Archive Stiftung Umwelteinsatz
Schweiz

Client:
Stiftung Umwelteinsatz Schweiz

The client organization is a small foundation that coordinates funding and support for such endeavors as alpine farming, alpine forests, and camps where participants undertake hands-on projects for the environment. The client wanted its annual report to communicate the foundation's creativity; cut through the everyday clutter of mail; and consist of absolutely environmentally safe materials.

The first step was to develop a concept that eliminated a mailing envelope (saving both costs and materials). The designers developed a simple flap, and an address sticker held everything together. Colors were chosen for warmth and earthiness, and inside stickers carry special messages—some essential, some entertaining— all giving the report a personal feel. Additional messages were occasionally placed as rubber stamps, and some type was set on a vintage typewriter, circa 1920. Because images the designers received would not reproduce well, they printed them in a rough dot-screen that complemented the unrefined feel of the report.

After testing an assortment of papers for environmental soundness, the designers chose an inexpensive brand that is used to line banana boxes. Then they further tested the effect of light on the paper's coloration. "Over a period of months, the paper darkened, but we welcomed the changes in tone, as they added to the warm feel of the piece," said Heinz Wild. The printer, confronted with this new paper, also conducted tests to see how the ink would hold. Inside pages were designed with cost-effective recycled paper, and cover and interior papers combined so they were aesthetically pleasing. This unique approach proved very successful, paying for itself as well as bringing a wealth of donations to the foundation.

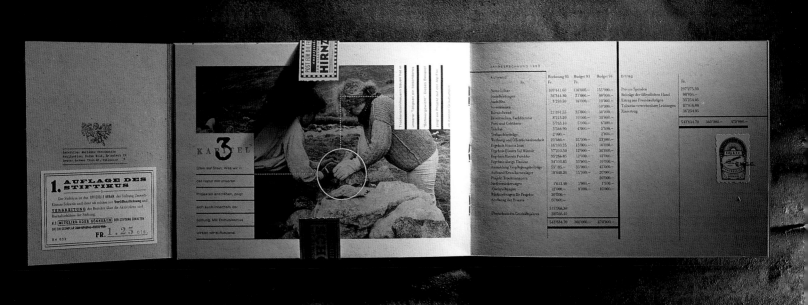

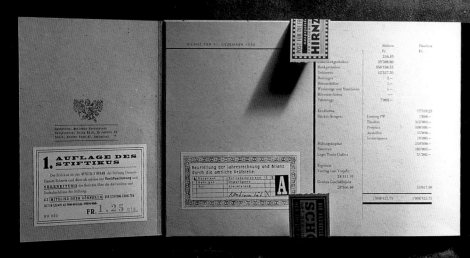

Bericht der Kontrollstelle:
Als Kontrollstelle Ihrer Stiftung haben wir
die auf den 31. Dezember 1993 abgeschlossene
Jahresrechnung geprüft. Wir stellen fest, dass
-die Bilanz und die Erfolgsrechnung, die
Spenden- und Einsatzstellenrechnung mit der
Buchhaltung übereinstimmen, - die Buchhaltung
ordnungsgemäss geführt ist, - bei der Dar-
stellung der Vermögenslage die gesetzlichen
Bewertungsgrundsätze sowie die Bestimmungen der
Stiftungsurkunde eingehalten sind. Aufgrund
der Ergebnisse unserer Prüfungen empfehlen wir
die vorliegende Bilanz zu genehmigen.
Reoplan Treuhand AG, Hans Kunz, H.R. Häfeli,
dipl. Bücherexperten. Bern, 13. 3. 1994.

INNOVATIVE
DESIGN
M·E·R·I·T
AWARDS

THESE SOLUTIONS AREN'T JUST UNIQUE—THEY'VE ACHIEVED UNIQUENESS WITHOUT EXPANDING THEIR COST BEYOND THE LIMIT OF "REASONABLE." WE INVITE YOU TO PAGE THROUGH THIS GROUP OF INNOVATIVE DESIGNS AND DISCOVER WHAT IS POSSIBLE WHEN YOU LET PURE CREATIVITY GUIDE THE IDEA, AND COMPREHENSION GUIDE THE EXECUTION.

<table>
<tr><td>

TOP

Project:
Shelley's Jellies Packaging

Design Firm:
Charney Design

Art Director:
Carol Inez Charney

Designer:
Carol Inez Charney

Illustrator:
Kim Ferrell

Writers:
Denise Ryan, Carol Inez Charney,
Shelley Ross

Client:
Shelley's Jellies

</td><td>

BOTTOM

Project:
Aid & Comfort Benefit Dinner
Packaging

Design Firm:
Hunt Weber Clark Associates

Art Director:
Nancy Hunt Weber

Designer:
Nancy Hunt Weber

Hand Stamping:
Friends of Hunt Weber Clark
Associates

Client:
Aid & Comfort Benefit
Concert/San Francisco Bay Area
Restaurants

</td></tr>
</table>

Project:
Alcatraz Ale Packaging

Design Firm:
Cahan & Associates

Art Director:
Bill Cahan

Designers:
Sharrie Brooks, Kevin Roberson

Client:
Boisset USA

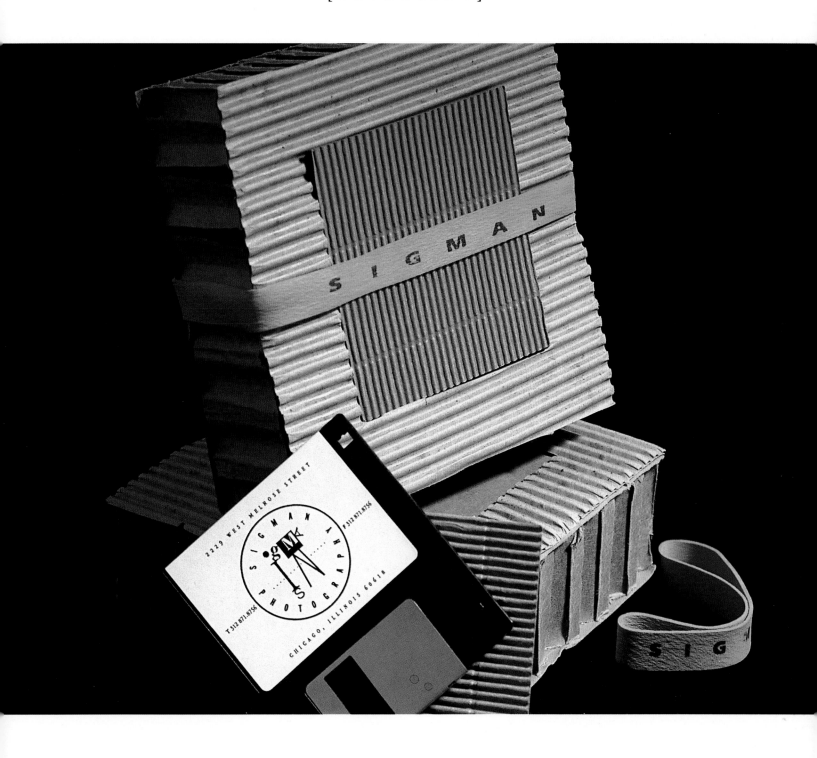

Project:
Sigman Photography Diskette
Package

Design Firm:
Nicholas Associates

Art Director:
Nicholas Sinadinos

Designers:
Nicholas Sinadinos, Scott Hardy

Client:
Gary Sigman Photography

Project:
Boots Bin Liners

Design Firm:
Lewis Moberly

Art Director:
Mary Lewis

Designer:
Bryan Clark

Client:
The Boots Company PLC

TOP LEFT
Project:
Prosperity Red Wine Label

Design Firm:
Mark Oliver, Inc.

Art Director:
Mark Oliver

Illustrator:
V. Courtlandt Johnson

Client:
Firestone Vineyard

BOTTOM LEFT
Project:
Adelphi Whisky

Design Firm:
Tayburn Ltd

Art Director:
Graham Scott

Designer:
Graham Scott

Calligrapher:
Robin Brellway

Client:
Adelphi Distillery

TOP RIGHT
Project:
Fresh Market Packaging

Design Firm:
Supon Design Group

Art Director:
Supon Phornirunlit

Designer:
Apisak "Eddie" Saibua

Illustrator:
Apisak "Eddie" Saibua

Client:
Fresh Market

BOTTOM RIGHT
Project:
EarthTime Watch Packaging

Design Firm:
Supon Design Group

Art Director:
Andrew Dolan

Designer:
Andrew Dolan

Illustrators:
Debbi Savitt (deer),
Andrew Dolan

Client:
Planet Called Earth

Project:
Dunlop Tuf Brand Identity

Design Firm:
Elton Ward Design

Art Director:
Steve Corman

Designer:
Chris DeLisen

Illustrator:
Andrew Schipp

Client:
Dunlop Footwear Australia

Project:
Print Communications Club
Paper Fair Bag

Design Firm:
CMF&Z Design

Art Director:
Brent Wirth

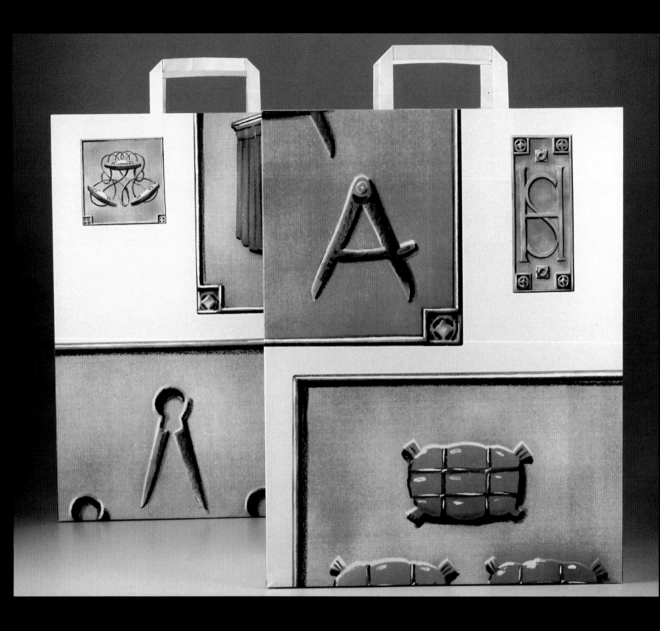

Project:
Heal's Carrier Bag

Design Firm:
Lewis Moberly

Art Director:
Mary Lewis

Designer:
Mary Lewis

Illustrator:
Geoffrey Appleton

Client:
Heal's

Project:
Areal Paper Bags

Design Firm:
Mário Aurélio & Associados

Art Director:
Mário Aurélio

Designers:
Mário Aurélio, Rosa Maia

Client:
Areal Editores

Project:
Esses-Samsung Corp.
Shopping Bag

Design Firm:
DooKim Design

Art Director:
Doo H. Kim

Designers:
Dongil Lee, Seunghee
Lee, Jongwha Ahn

Agency:
Cheil Comm./
CI Team

Client:
Esses-Samsung Corp.

Project:
Community Partnership of
Santa Clara County
Stationery

Design Firm:
Earl Gee Design

Art Director:
Fani Chung

Designer:
Fani Chung

Illustrator:
Fani Chung

Client:
Community Partnership of
Santa Clara County

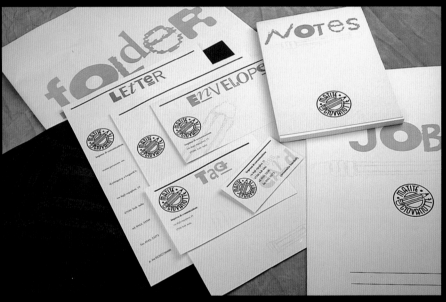

TOP

Project:
1647 Ltd Corporate Identity
& Branding

Design Firm:
The Green House

Art Director:
Judi Green

Designer:
James Bell

Client:
Dawn French, Helen Teague

BOTTOM

Project:
Agency Stationery

Design Firm:
Matite Giovanotte

Art Director:
Barbara Longiardi

Designer:
Giovanni Pizzigati

Illustrator:
Barbara Casadei

Copywriter:
Antonella Bandoli

Client:
Matite Giovanotte

Project:
Tabula Tua Retail Identity

Design Firm:
Monnens-Addis Design

Art Director:
Joanne Hom, Steven Addis

Designer:
Joanne Hom

Client:
Tabula Tua

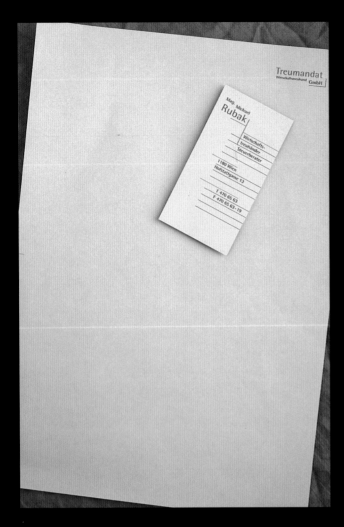

Project:
Treumandat Stationery

Design Firm:
Atelier Heider

Art Director:
Clemens Heider

Designer:
Clemens Heider

Client:
Mag. Michael Rubak

Project:
Sheehan Identity

Design Firm:
Sheehan Design

Art Director:
Jamie Sheehan

Designer:
Jamie Sheehan

Illustrator:
Jamie Sheehan

Client:
Sheehan Design

Project:
UNESCO-Projekt-Schulen

Design Firm:
Kleiner & Bold

Designer:
Tammo F. Bruns, Frank
Schulte, Karsten
Unterberger

Illustrator:
Andreas Weiss

Client:
Bundeskoordination der
UNESCO-Projekt-Schulen

Project:
Profit Retention Concepts
Brochure

Design Firm:
Melia Design Group

Art Director:
Mark Silvers

Designer:
Mark Silvers

Client:
Profit Retention Concepts

Project:
Sitz & Co. Stationery

Design Firm:
Denis Schwarz

Art Director:
Denis Schwarz

Designer:
Denis Schwarz

Client:
Sitz & Co.

Project:
Craig Singleton Hollomon
Architects Stationery

Design Firm:
Communication Arts Company

Art Director:
Hilda Staussowen

Designer:
Hilda Staussowen

Client:
Craig Singleton Hollomon
Architects

Project:
Image Source Identity

Design Firm:
Rauscher Design Inc.

Designer:
Russ Jackson

Photographer:
Micheal Reilly

Client:
Image Source Inc.

Project:
Zandhoeven Chocolate
Company Identity

Design Firm:
Thibault Paolini Design
Associates

Art Director:
Judith Paolini

Designer:
Judith Paolini

Illustrator:
Barbara Emmons

Client:
Zandhoeven Chocolate
Company

Sabine Carbon
Journalistin

Sonnenallee 29, 1000 Berlin 44
Telefon: 030 6235591

Sabine Carbon
Journalistin

Sonnenallee 29, 1000 Berlin 44
Telefon: 030 6235591

Project:
Sabine Carbon Stationery

Design Firm:
Pentagram

Art Director:
Justus Oehler

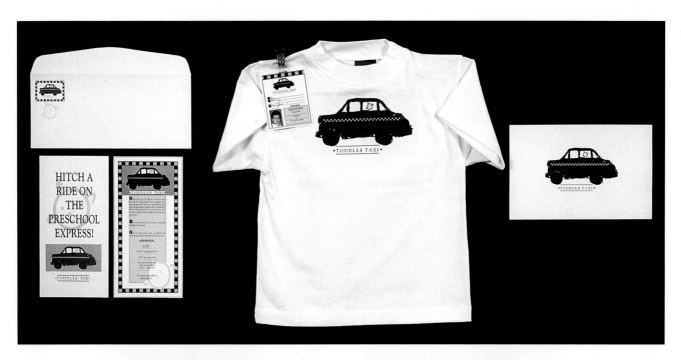

TOP
Project:
Toddler Taxi Marketing Design

Design Firm:
Dutchmill Design

Art Director:
Patti J. Lachance

Designer:
Patti J. Lachance

Illustrator:
Patti J. Lachance

Client:
Toddler Taxi

BOTTOM
Project:
Full Moon Foods Identity

Design Firm:
Sackett Design Associates

Art Director:
Mark Sackett

Designers:
Mark Sackett, Wayne Sakamoto

Illustrator:
Mark Sackett

Client:
Full Moon Foods & Mercantile

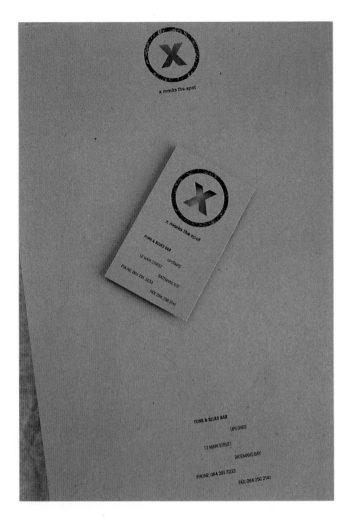

Project:
X Marks The Spot–
Funk and Blues Bar

Design Firm:
Wingrove & Wingrove
Design Studio

Art Directors:
Damian Monaghan, Ian Wingrove,
Rosie Wingrove

Designer:
Damian Monaghan

Client:
Coburn Construction Pty Ltd

Project:
Junk Jewels Letterhead

Design Firm:
Communication Arts
Company

Designer:
Ashley Barron

Client:
Malcolm and Vivian White

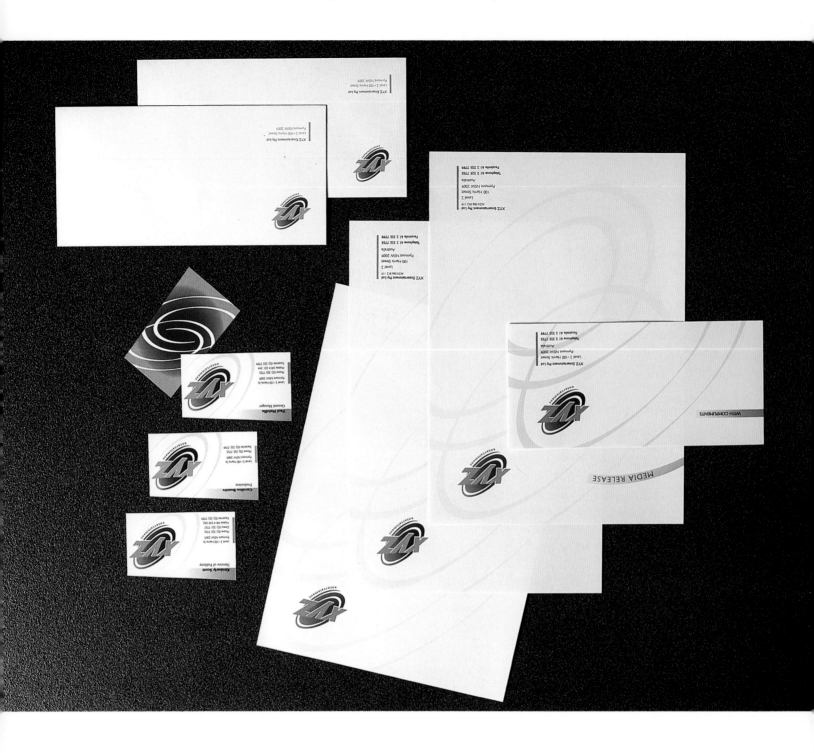

Project:
XYZ Entertainment Letterhead

Design Firm:
Spatchurst Design Associates

Art Director:
Steven Joseph

Designers:
Meryl Blondell, Ingo Voss

Client:
XYZ Entertainment

Project:
Crystalvision Stationery

Design Firm:
Wonder Studio

Art Director:
Howard Yang

Designer:
Sherri Yu

Photographer:
Howard Yang

Client:
Crystalvision Film
Productions

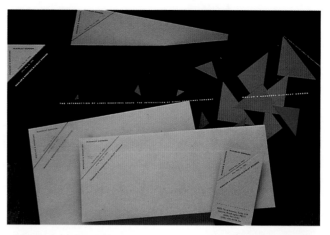

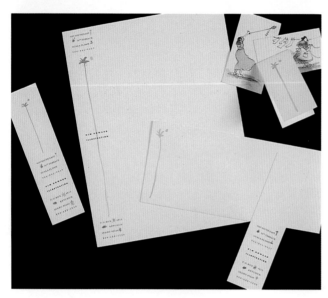

TOP LEFT

Project:
Corporate Identity For Boonoke
Fashion Label

Design Firm:
Gillian Allan

Art Director:
Gillian Allan

Designer:
Gillian Allan

Client:
Isis Design/The Great Australian
Jumper Company

BOTTOM LEFT

Project:
Kim Howard Stationery

Design Firm:
Sackett Design Associates

Art Director:
Mark Sackett

Designers:
Mark Sackett, James Sakamoto

Illustrator:
Kim Howard

Client:
Kim Howard

TOP RIGHT

Project:
Mahlum & Nordfors McKinley
Gordon Transitional Stationery

Design Firm:
Hornall Anderson Design Works,
Inc.

Art Director:
Jack Anderson

Designers:
Jack Anderson, Scott Eggers,
Leo Raymundo

Client:
Mahlum & Nordfors McKinley
Gordon

BOTTOM RIGHT

Project:
USABA Stationery

Design Firm:
After Hours Creative

Art Director:
After Hours Creative

Designer:
After Hours Creative

Client:
United States Association
of Blind Athletes

LEFT

Project:
Big Design Group Letterhead

Design Firm:
Big Design Group

Art Director:
Mark Wilcox

Designer:
Mark Wilcox

Client:
Big Design Group

RIGHT

Project:
Montana Bar & Restaurant
Identity

Design Firm:
The Green House

Art Director:
Judi Green

Designer:
Victor Liew

Client:
Alpine Investments Ltd

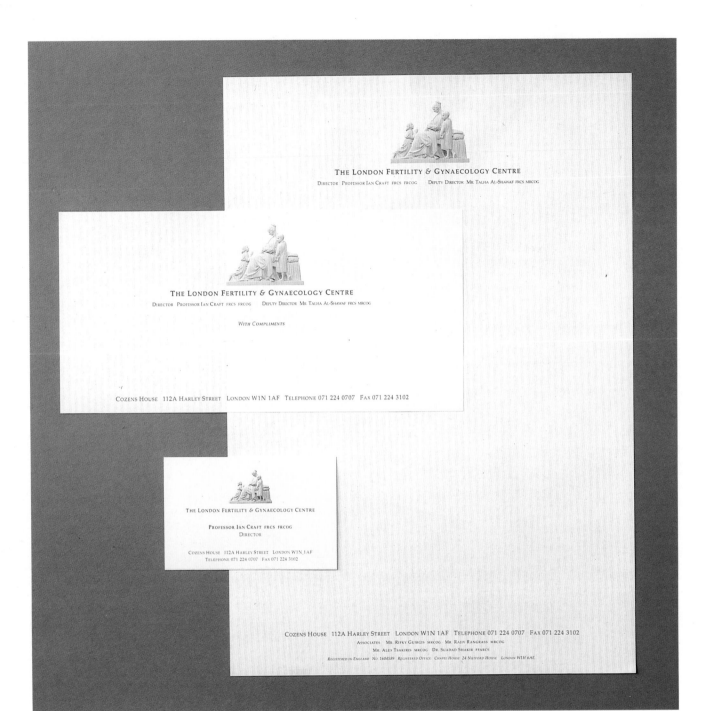

Project:
The London Fertility and
Gynecology Centre

Design Firm:
The Team Design
Consultant

Art Director:
Richard Ward

Designer:
Richard Ward

Client:
The London Fertility and
Gynecology Centre

[N E W S L E T T E R S]

Project:
"Inside EMC" Newsletter

Design Firm:
EMC Marketing and
Advertising Inc.

Art Director:
Vanessa Weber

Designer:
Vanessa Weber

Copywriters:
Jill Boarts, Mary Kukovich

Client:
Education Management

Project:
Science Museum
Education Pack

Design Firm:
Lewis Moberly

Art Director:
Bryan Clark

Designer:
Robert Howsam

Illustrator:
Martin Chatterton

Client:
The Science Museum

the Atlanta Opera news

Winter 1995   Volume 10 No. 1

Moorish Magic, Devilish Doings and an Egyptian Jewel

ON SEPTEMBER 5, 1994, The Atlanta Opera closed its most successful season to date with every performance selling to capacity. Each night, last-minute ticket buyers were turned away, audiences applauded and critics roared. Opera-goers traveled from the splendor of Turandot's Chinese palace to the mysterious ruins of Leila's Brahmin temple to the quiet majesty of Norma's sacred oak. So, one might ask, how will The Atlanta Opera top that in '95?

...By delivering all of the grand and glorious musical theatre that Atlanta Opera-goers have come to expect amid the fairy-tale splendor of the fabulous Fox Theatre! That's right. While Symphony Hall gets a face-lift, The Atlanta Opera moves its mainstage performances to the Fox Theatre, perhaps the greatest surviving example of the fantastic movie palaces of the 1920s and the ideal setting for the wondrous, rich and grand art form known as opera. And no two operas in the repertoire are grander than those lined up for the 1995 season: Gounod's soul-stirring Faust and Verdi's heart-pounding Aida. Here are two of the most spectacular and loved operas ever written, filled with some of the most soaring and exquisite melodies ever composed. From Faust's "Soldiers' Chorus" to Aida's "Triumphal March," the 1995 season promises to be the most glorious yet.

FAUST June 1 & 3

While nearly two dozen composers have adapted Goethe's Faust to the musical stage, it was surely in Charles Gounod that the classic tale found its finest and most ennobling voice. Having lost his faith in both science and love, Faust, the aging philosopher, makes a demonic pact with Satan in order to regain lost youth and to secure the love of the beautiful Marguerite. Ultimately, his deal with the Devil destroys the innocent girl and condemns Faust to eternal damnation.

Our cast will feature tenor Allan Glassman as Faust, bass Kenneth Cox as Mephistopheles, soprano Ai-Lan Zhu as Marguerite, Haijing Fu as Valentine and mezzo-soprano Deidra Palmour as Siebel.

AIDA August 31 & September 2

Giuseppe Verdi's Aida is Grand Opera with a capital 'G'! The beloved and tragic tale of the enslaved Ethiopian princess and her valiant Egyptian lover comes to life with some of Verdi's most beautiful melodies and awe-inspiring spectacle. What more need be said!

Our cast will feature Camellia Johnson as Aida, Greek mezzo-soprano Markella Hatziano as Amneris, tenor Stephen O'Mara as Radames, bass-baritone Hao Jiang Tian as Ramfis and baritone Mark Rucker as Amonasro.

So join us beneath the glow of the lanterns, under the stars and Moorish turrets of the fabulous Fox and be transported on the wings of song to the medieval Germany of Doctor Georg Faustus, a world delicately balanced between science and faith where the Devil lies in wait around every corner, and to Aida's Egypt where pharaohs and priests wage their wars amidst the monumental pyramids and towering temples of a mysterious lost civilization.

The Fabulous Fox will be home for The Atlanta Opera's '95 season. *Photo: Kevin Rose*

GIVING THE DEVIL HIS DUE

AS THE MIDDLE AGES GAVE WAY TO THE RENAISSANCE, THERE APPEARED ON THE SCENE A HISTORICAL PERSONAGE BY THE NAME OF GEORG FAUSTUS, AROUND WHOM CRYSTALLIZED THE THEMES OF A PERPLEXING DILEMMA THAT HAD HAD ITS SEEDS IN THE ANCIENT STORY OF ADAM AND EVE.

The tale of Eve's disobedience needs little retelling. God forbids Adam and Eve to eat "the fruit of the tree which is in the midst of the garden"; the serpent tempts Eve to do otherwise; she eats of the fruit. Retribution, of course, follows immediately: Adam and Eve are expelled from Eden, and a flaming sword bars their return. Literally speaking, human kind did not want much time before testing the limitations put upon them by their humanity.

Despite the attempts of succeeding generations to blame her for mankind's fall from grace and loss of Paradise, Eve may be seen as an early example of humanity at its noblest, eternally searching for truth in the face of uncertainty, pulled between the desires of faith and the quest for knowledge, yearning to know good and evil, and striving to become like its creator, even at the expense of defying him. Though the word would not exist for many centuries, Eve might in this sense be called truly "Faustian."

Georg Faustus, it could be said, was the spiritual heir of this Humanistic view of Eve's rebellion. His lifetime spanned the years from the late fifteenth century until 1540, an era when two powerful world views coexisted and vied for dominance. Astrology and alchemy were becoming astronomy and chemistry, religion was challenged by rationalism, blind faith in the priesthood was undermined by Luther's translation of the Bible, whose wide dissemination was made possible by that new

by Robert A. Glick

Goethe's doomed Dr. Faust finally found glorious expression in the noble melodies of composer Charles Gounod.

invention, the printing press. And even as education was becoming much more available and many new areas of study were possible, the University of Cracow still offered a degree in Black Magic.

A graduate of that program, the historical Faustus traveled throughout German-speaking Europe, introducing himself in 1506 as "Master George Sabellicus, the younger Faustus, fountain head of conjurers of the dead, reader in the stars, second mage, seer of the future, conjurer of air, conjurer of fire, and skilled in the art of water." In 1507 he was calling himself the "Heidelberg demigod" and in 1513 he was lecturing at the University of Erfurt, according to reports criticizing his classes in Homer by conjuring up the classical heroes before his students' eyes.

Faustus became famous for both his magic and his dissolute lifestyle. On one occasion he was visited by a Franciscan monk, who sought to convince him to reform his ways. Faustus solemnly declared that he could not, that he had sold his soul to the Devil in exchange for his knowledge. When the monk assured him that God's mercy was infinite and that a mass could purify him, Faustus replied: "Mass this, mass that: the devil has fairly kept what he promised me and therefore I intend to keep fairly what I promised and signed away to him." Whether Faustus intended to be taken literally or whether he was merely trying to get rid of a bothersome visitor is unknown, but such contracts were widely believed in the period. His legend grew, abetted by his claim of the supernatural and assistance of a spiritus familiaris, a kind of demonic version of Aladdin's genie.

In Wittenburg during the 1520s, no less than Philip Melanchthon, Luther's humanist friend and the most respected Protestant leader after Luther's death, associated with Faustus and chronicled his feats of magic. By 1540, Faustus had returned to his native village and died, undoubtedly in a bad

spiritual condition as his corpse was discovered face down, a sure sign of damnation. His black dog, reputed sometimes to serve him in human form, had disappeared. After his death, Faustus' reputation grew and numerous reports, items of gossip, legends and perhaps some historical facts about him and many others were added to the Faust story, to be printed by Johann Spies in 1587 and known as the *Faustbuch* or *Faust Book*.

The work was an immediate bestseller, going through 16 printings within the next two years. Almost immediately, the *Faust Book* appeared in English translation, but with some modifications. Even though called *The History of the Damnable Life and Deserved Death of Doctor John Faustus*, the author, one "P.F., Gentleman," is not quite so critical of the figure, damnable though he may be. Perhaps this reveals a more English willingness, only shortly after the reign of Henry VIII, to accept rebellion against the church. Sometime between 1588 and 1594, this work and conception of the Faustus figure became the source of Christopher Marlowe's play, *The Tragical History of the Life and Death of Doctor Faustus*.

Marlowe's work follows the general outlines of the English *Faust Book*, yet there is a grandeur and nobility to his hero that is lacking in the earlier versions. Undoubtedly, this is in part due to what Ben Jonson referred to as "Marlowe's mighty line," that is, the sheer power and magnificence of Marlowe's language. But it is also partially due to the higher sense of purpose Faustus has in turning to the black arts. Displaying a Renaissance desire for the unlimited expansion of human knowledge and power, he decides to reject religion and turn to magic. In a passage almost invoking the image of Eve as she reached for the forbidden fruit, he says: "A sound magician is a mighty god: / Here, Faustus, try thy brains to gain a deity!"

In spite of his pact with Mephistophilis to exchange his soul for 24 years of "all voluptuousness," Marlowe's Faustus continually intends to use his powers for mankind's advancement, to

continued on page 7

the Atlanta Opera news

WINTER 1995
VOLUME 10 No. 1

FAUST
GOUNOD'S MASTERPIECE OPENS THE SEASON ON JUNE 1 & 3 AT THE FABULOUS FOX THEATRE.

AIDA
VERDI'S BLOCKBUSTER EPIC COMES ALIVE ON THE FOX THEATRE STAGE ON AUGUST 31 AND SEPTEMBER 2.

1995 SEASON PREVIEW ISSUE

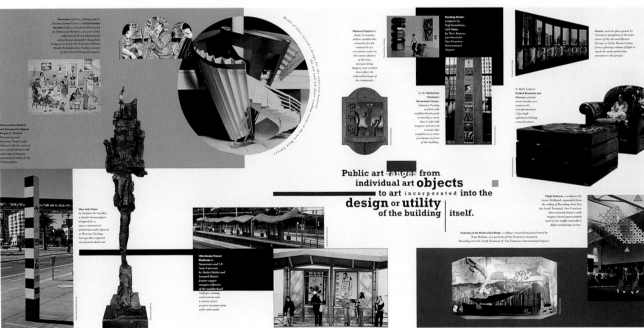

Project:
San Francisco Art Commission
Public Art Program Brochure

Design Firm:
Earl Gee Design

Art Director:
Earl Gee

Designer:
Earl Gee

Photographers:
Lenny Limjoco and others

Client:
San Francisco Art Commission

Project:
Smoke-Free Policy for Schools

Design Firm:
Asprey Di Donato Design

Art Director:
Asprey Di Donato Design

Designer:
Asprey Di Donato Design

Illustrator:
Peter Asprey

Client:
The Quit Campaign

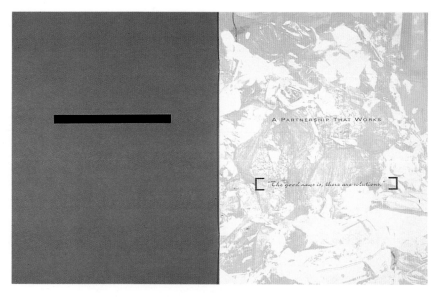

TOP

Project:
Metro Waste Authority (MWA)
Corporate Brochure

Design Firm:
CMF&Z Design

Art Director:
Pat Fultz

Designer:
Pat Fultz

Copywriter:
Mark Lunde

Photographer:
Andrea Bocci

Client:
Metro Waste Authority

BOTTOM

Project:
Jugendkulturaustausch "Stuttgart
Meets San Francisco" Brochure

Designer:
Olaf Becker

Illustrator:
Olaf Becker

Client:
Cumulus Kulturbüro

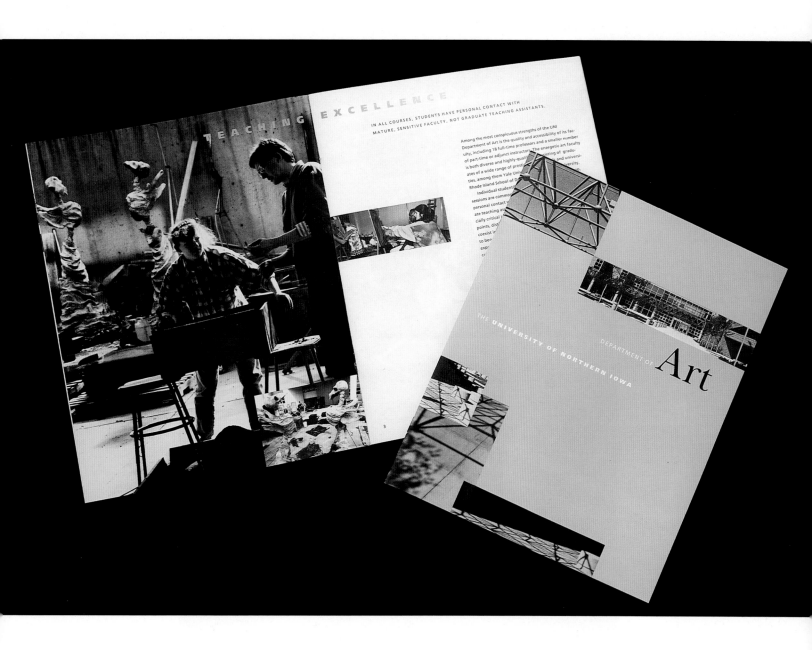

Project:
UNI Art Department
Brochure

Art Director:
Philip Fass

Designer:
Philip Fass

Copywriter:
Roy Behrens

Client:
University of Northern Iowa
Department of Art

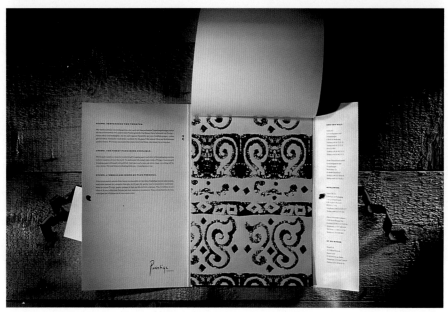

Project:
Stewo Prestige
Promotional Brochure

Design Firm:
Wild & Frey

Art Director:
Lucia Frey

Designers:
Lucia Frey, Heinz Wild

Photographer:
Frank Tomio

Client:
Stewo AG, Geschenkpapiere
und Verpackuneen

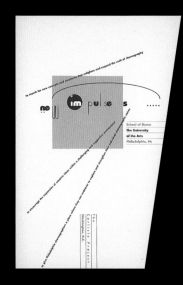

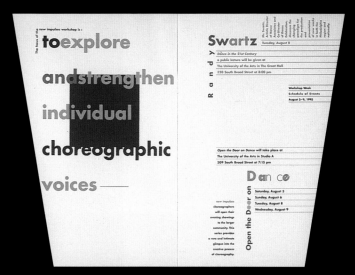

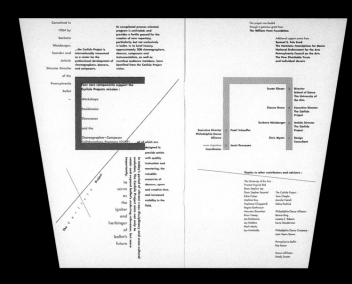

Project:
New Impulses Brochure

Design Firm:
The Office of Mayer & Myers

Art Director:
Nancy Mayer

Designer:
Chris Myers

Clients:
School of Dance,
The University of the Arts
(Philadelphia), and
The Carlisle Project
(Washington, D.C.)

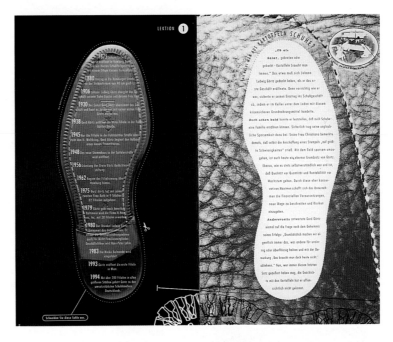

TOP

Project:
Görtz "The Company"
Brochure

Design Firm:
Springer & Jacoby

Art Director:
Antje Hedde

Designer:
Antje Hedde

Photographers:
Witte & Bergling,
Astrid Grosser

Finished Drawing:
Shoshanah Miller

Client:
Ludwig Görtz GmbH

BOTTOM

Project:
Görtz "The Stuff" Brochure

Design Firm:
Springer & Jacoby

Art Director:
Antje Hedde

Designer:
Antje Hedde

Photographer:
Witte & Bergling

Client:
Ludwig Görtz GmbH

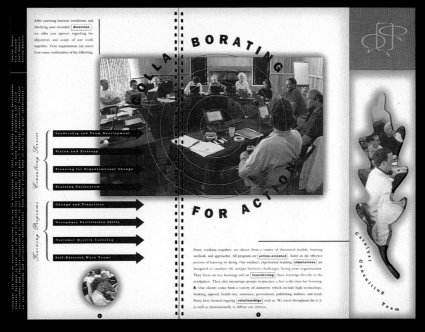

Project:
Catalyst Consulting Team
Brochure

Design Firm:
Earl Gee Design

Art Director:
Earl Gee

Designers:
Earl Gee, Fani Chung

Illustrator:
Earl Gee

Photographers:
Geoffrey Nelson,
Lenny Lind

Project:
Nike Components Brochure

Design Firm:
Matite Giovanotte

Art Directors:
Giovanni Pizzigati,
Antonella Bandoli

Junior Art Director:
Barbara Casadei

Designer:
Barbara Longiardi

Photographer:
Werther Scudellari

Client:
Nike Italy

Project:
Selecting a College:
Fact vs. Fiction Brochure

Design Firm:
Office of Publications,
Seton Hall University

Art Director:
Jean Smith

Designer:
Jean Smith

Printer:
Hatteras Press

Client:
Seton Hall University

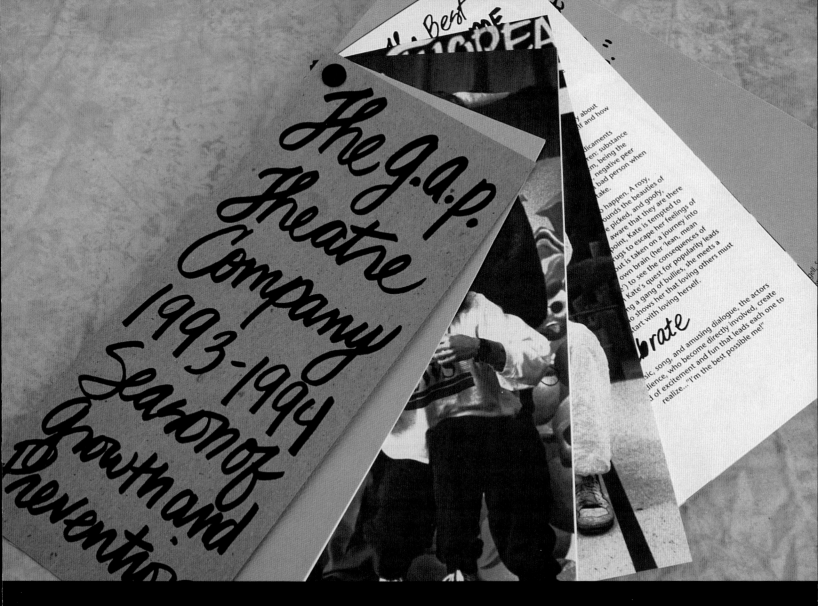

The G.A.P. Theatre Company 1993-1994 Season of Growth and Prevention

Project:
The G.A.P. Theatre Company
Ticket Brochure

Design Firm:
Hansen Design Company

Art Director:
Pat Hansen

Designer:
Pat Hansen

Photographer:
Chris Bennion

Printer:
Trojan Lithograph, Adhesa Plate

Client:
The G.A.P. (Growth and
Prevention) Theatre Company

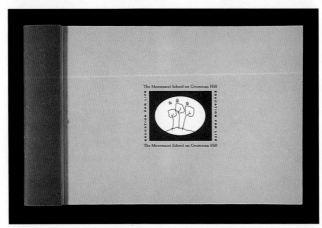

Project:
SGC Benefits Brochure

Design Firm:
Toni Schowalter Design

Art Director:
Toni Schowalter

Designer:
Toni Schowalter

Illustrator:
Toni Schowalter Design

Client:
Supermarkets General Corp.

Project:
The Montessori School Brochure,
Education for Life

Design Firm:
The Q Design Group Ltd

Art Director:
Charyn RS Atkin

Designer:
Christine DiGuiseppi

Photographer:
Dru Nadler

Client:
The Montessori School on
Grumman Hill

Project:
Ontario Fishing Guide

Design Firm:
2 Dimensions Inc. Advertising
By Design

Art Director:
Kam Wai Yu

Designer:
Kam Wai Yu

Illustrator:
Raffi Anderian

Client:
Ontario Ministry of Tourism

Where can DYNEX help?

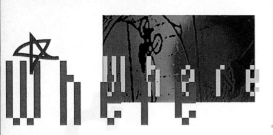

✦ ...where it makes dollars and sense for you!

Sales Support — high-impact, easy-to-transport sales presentations

Lead Generation — traffic-stopping trade show and in-store kiosks

Performance and Learning — transforming existing presentations to interactive formats

Overhead Reduction — converting classroom training to individualized learning

Cost Containment — developing tools for distance training

Project:
Ontario College of Art
Admissions Brochure

Design Firm:
Overdrive Design Ltd.

Art Director:
Jay Wilson

Designer:
Jay Wilson

Illustrator:
Jay Wilson

Copywriters/Editors:
Deborah Perry,
Michael Waldin

Client:
Ontario College of Art

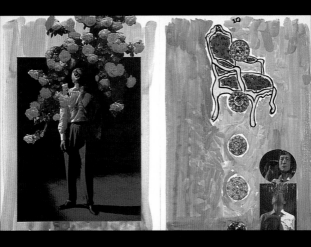

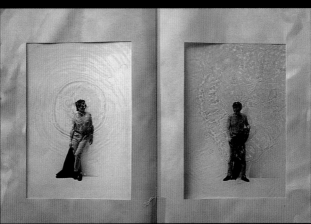

Project:
Eikichi Yazawa Tour Pamphlet

Design Firm:
Kenzo Izutani Office Corporation

Art Director:
Ken'zo Izutani

Designers:
Kenzo Izutani, Aki Hirai

Project:
Boy Scouts of America
1994 Annual Report

Design Firm:
John Brady Design Consultants

Art Director:
John Brady

Designer:
Paula Madden

Photographer:
Tom Gigliotti

Assembler:
Emil Ratkovich

Client:
Greater Pittsburgh Council

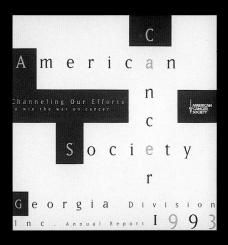

American Cancer Society

Channeling Our Efforts
to win the war on cancer

AMERICAN CANCER SOCIETY

Georgia Division

Inc. Annual Report **1993**

Skin Cancer

"The Chatham County unit happened to make skin cancer
a priority in 1993. If it weren't for that,

I wouldn't have been so
alert to the spot
on Kris' back

and she might not have made it."

Skin Cancer

"I've never been more
thankful that I work at the
American Cancer Society,

and that the Chatham County unit happened
to make skin cancer a priority in 1993."

— Sylvia Manes, Savannah

Sylvia Manes and
daughter Kris

Seven-year-old Kris Manes got
a bad sunburn when she was
four. It left some large freckles
and a suspicious looking spot
on her back. Because her mom, Sylvia
Manes, program director for the Chatham County
unit, was in the midst of a comprehensive, year-long
skin cancer project, she recognized Kris' spot from
the melanoma photos. Kris was diagnosed with Stage
2 melanoma, and subsequently had three operations
during which nine lesions were removed — one was
malignant and six were premalignant. "I've worked
for the Society for seven years, but all my knowledge was gone when I heard the word melanoma,"
says Sylvia. Though skin cancer in children is rare,
and doctors don't link Kris' sunburn with her diag-
nosis, Sylvia remains a believer in prevention. Kris,
who's on the Savannah Swim Team, says it best:
"Wear sunscreen, because what I went through felt
really bad."

1993 Skin Cancer
Control Highlights

· Released three new age-specific videos and accom-
panying materials aimed at teachers and students,
courtesy of the Texas, Illinois and Wisconsin
divisions.

· Developing, in conjunction with AARP, an inter-
generational sun protection program aimed
at grandparents.

Skin Cancer Trends

· Overexposure to the sun is the most common
cause of skin cancer.

· Skin cancer is one of the fastest growing
types of cancer — 850 cases were diagnosed
in Georgia in 1993.

· It's also one of the most curable; when detect-
ed and treated early, the survival rate for
localized malignant melanoma is 91 percent.

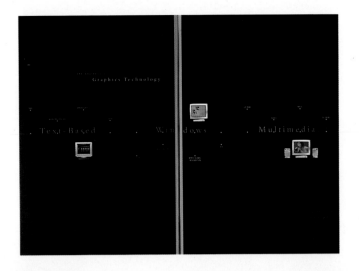

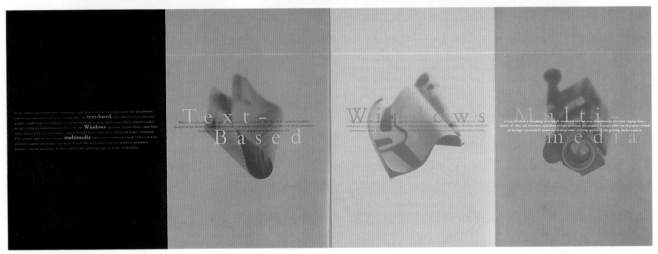

Project:
Trident Microsystems
Annual Report

Design Firm:
Cahan & Associates

Art Director:
Bill Cahan

Designer:
Bob Dinetz

Photographer:
Holly Stewart

Client:
Trident Microsystems, Inc.

TOP
Project:
ConnieLee Annual Report

BOTTOM
Project:
USW Biennual Review

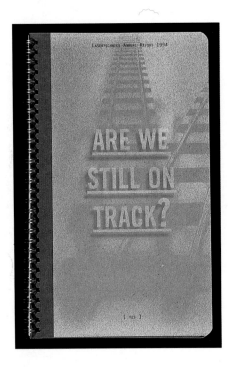

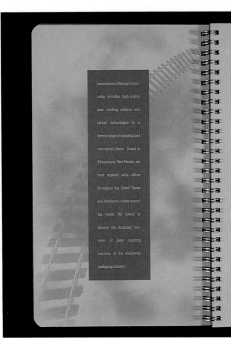

TOP

Project:
Gilead Sciences Annual Report

Design Firm:
Cahan & Associates

Art Director:
Bill Cahan

Designer:
Kevin Roberson

Photographer:
Christine Alicino

Client:
Gilead Sciences

BOTTOM

Project:
Lasertechnics Annual Report

Design Firm:
Vaughn Wedeen Creative, Inc.

Art Director:
Steve Wedeen

Designer:
Steve Wedeen

Photographer:
Dave Nufer

Computer Production:
Adabel Allen Kaskiewicz

Client:
Lasertechnics, Inc.

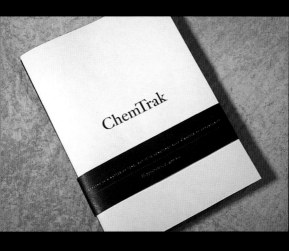

AccuMeter

[ACTUAL SIZE]

ChemTrak was founded to bring healthcare closer to the patient by significantly changing the way many *in vitro* diagnostic tests (i.e., tests performed on blood, urine and other specimens taken from the body) are performed. Currently, most diagnostic testing involves multiple steps in clinical laboratories. Trained technicians must receive and process a specimen, measure its volume, add reagents, use sophisticated machinery to determine results and get that information back to the medical professional who conveys the information to the patient, all of which typically takes at least 1 - 2 days.

But ChemTrak's AccuMeter® technology provides the same information conveniently, easily and in minutes.

The patented, noninstrumented, palm-size AccuMeter cassette system is an enabling technology expected to be

USES UNPROCESSED SAMPLES

11 U.S. PATENTS ISSUED AND 9 PENDING

VERSATILE TECHNOLOGY

Cholesterol

The first AccuMeter product is a single-use, whole blood-based cassette that reads much like a thermometer to quantify total cholesterol levels in about 15 minutes.

An application has been submitted to the FDA for the company's second product, the professional market AccuMeter High-Density Lipoprotein test. The format of this test is similar to the total cholesterol test and ChemTrak plans to develop the HDL cholesterol self-test for the worldwide OTC market.

Cholesterol is comprised of HDL, LDL and very low-density lipoprotein (precursors of LDL) cholesterol. Testing for total cholesterol is sufficient for screening patients for overall risk of heart disease. However, in cases of borderline-high and high total cholesterol an elevated percentage of HDL cholesterol indicates a lower patient risk profile.

ADD BLOOD DROPS

PULL TAB TO BEGIN PROCESS

READ RESULTS LIKE A THERMOMETER

Project:
ChemTrak Annual Report

Design Firm:
Cahan & Associates

Art Director:
Bill Cahan

Project:
Boy Scouts of America Annual
Report 1993

TOP

Project:
COR Therapeutics Annual Report

Design Firm:
Cahan & Associates

Art Director:
Bill Cahan

Designer:
Bob Dinetz

Illustrator:
Joel Nakamura

Photographer:
Jock McDonald

Client:
COR Therapeutics

BOTTOM

Project:
Unity Temple Restoration
Foundation Annual Report

Design Firm:
Nicholas Associates

Art Director:
Nicholas Sinadinos

Designers:
Nicholas Sinadinos, Carol Crews

Illustrator:
Carol Crews

Client:
Unity Temple Restoration
Foundation

TOP
Project:
Textile Exchange Catalogue

Design Firm:
Wöhlnick Design

Art Director:
Karel Wöhlnick

Designer:
Karel Wöhlnick

Client:
Australian Textile Exchange Group

BOTTOM
Project:
Vestige of Function Catalog

Design Firm:
Asprey Di Donato Design

Art Director:
Asprey Di Donato Design

Designer:
Asprey Di Donato Design

Photographer:
Stephen Jennings

Client:
Royal Melbourne Institute
of Technology

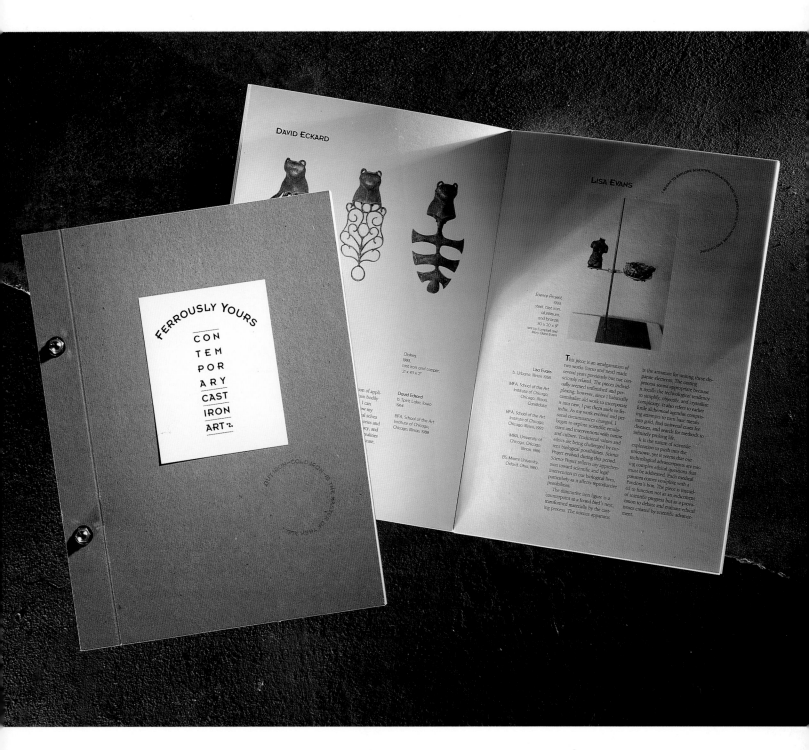

Project:
Cast Iron Catalog

Design Firm:
Weaver Design

Designer:
Marie Weaver

Editor:
Antoinette Spanos
Nordan

Client:
University of Alabama at
Birmingham Visual Arts
Gallery

Project:
Inmotion Dealer Catalog

Design Firm:
Richard Endly Design, Inc.

Art Director:
Richard Endly

Designer:
Keith Wolf

Illustrator:
Keith Wolf

Photographer:
Richard Endly Design, Inc.

Copywriter:
Mike Gibbs

Client:
Inmotion

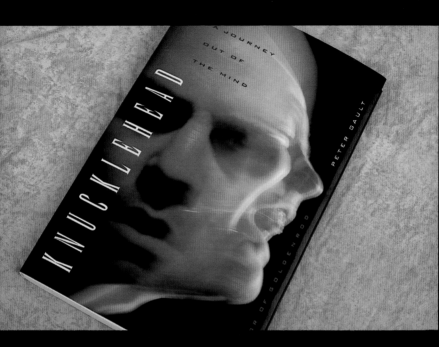

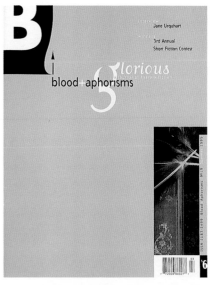

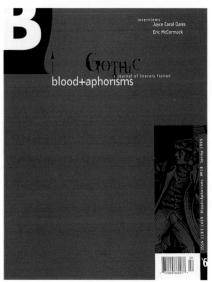

LEFT
Project:
Bauen an Zürich Book

Design Firm:
BBV Prof. M. Baviera

Art Director:
Michael Baviera

Designers:
Hans-Georg Köhl, Siegrun Nuber

Photographer:
Eduard Hueber

Client:
Bauamt II der Stadt Zürich

RIGHT
Project:
Blood + Aphorisms Literary
Magazine

Design Firm:
Overdrive Design Ltd.

Art Director:
Jay Wilson

Designer:
Jay Wilson

Client:
Blood + Aphorisms

'All the questions I needed answering when I was preparing for the National Competition, I find covered in this handbook'. John Patterson

This handbook was written using the detailed advice given to us by previous Work Skill Australia finalists, judges, trainers and committee members. It brings together their collective wisdom about what enhances effective performance in Work Skill Australia National Competitions. **This package is to help you prepare for your National Competition. Read the text, do the exercises, don't judge it by its size but by its value. Don't put it in the cupboard, go out and do it, be a winner!**

Life is all about meeting new challenges and gaining experience as you go. If your instincts indicate to you a certain direction, do everything you can to rea... full po...

The Regional Competitor, Congratulations! You are one of a special group of young people selected to join the CLIP program. By your performances so far you have already demonstrated that you have the skills to achieve at a superior level. But let's pause for a moment. Can you imagine sportsperson competing at a national or internatio... without a formal training program to help th... goals? **Of course not!** Well, you will soon be a National... champions. The h... been developed from... But it has... the...

Project:
Clip Handbook

Design Firm:
How Graphic Design

Art Directors:
Jon Howe,
Gillian Allan

Designers:
Jon Howe,
Gillian Allan

Client:
Work Skill Australia
Foundation

Project:
Qwerty, Issue Five

Design Firm:
The Letterbox

Art Director:
Stephen Banham

Designer:
Stephen Banham

Client:
The Letterbox

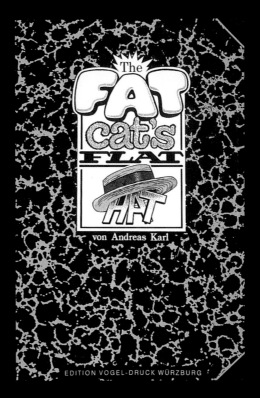

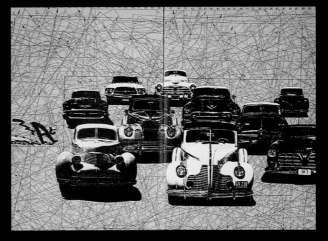

Project:
The Fat Cat's
Flat Hat Book

Design Firm:
Karl Design

Art Director:
Andreas Karl

Designer:
Andreas Karl

Illustrator:
Andreas Karl

Client:
Karl Design

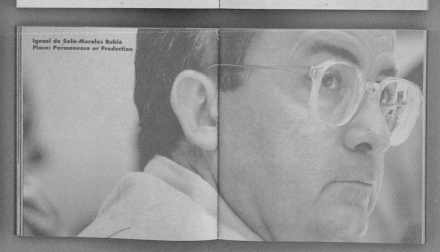

Project:
Anyone and *Anywhere*
Books

Design Firm:
Vignelli Associates

Art Director:
Massimo Vignelli

Designers:
Massimo Vignelli,
Judy Gleib, Sabu Kosho

Photographer:
Luca Vignelli

Client:
Anyone Corporation/
Rizzoli

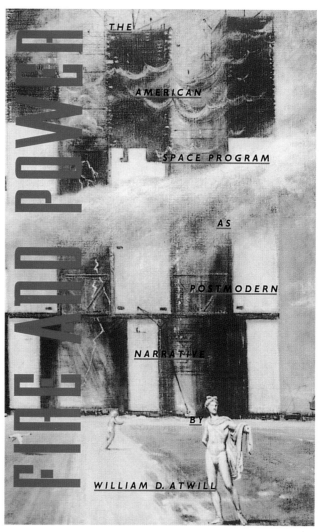

Project:
Stop the Violence! Book Cover

Design Firm:
Tim Girvin Design, Inc.

Art Director:
Tim Girvin

Designer:
Stephen Pannone

Illustrator:
Tim Girvin

Client:
Michelle Clise

Project:
Fire and Power Book Jacket

Design Firm:
The University of Georgia Press

Art Director:
Mary Mendell

Designer:
Mary Mendell

Painting:
"The New Olympus"
by Alden Wicks

Client:
The University of Georgia Press

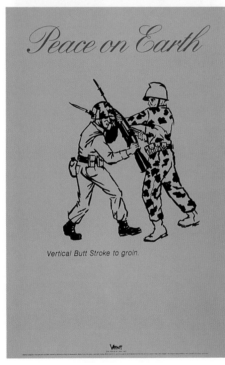

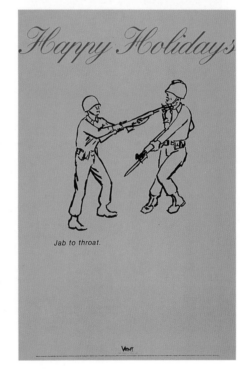

TOP

Project:
Continuing Professional
Development Posters

Design Firm:
Grundy & Northedge

Art Director:
Peter Grundy

Designer:
Peter Grundy

Illustrator:
Peter Grundy

Client:
Chartered Society of Designers,
London

BOTTOM

Project:
Vent Holiday Posters

Design Firm:
After Hours Creative

Art Director:
After Hours Creative

Designer:
After Hours Creative

Illustrator:
U.S. Marine Corps

Client:
Vent

Project:
Juneteenth Heritage Festival Poster

Design Firm:
Walsh Associates

Art Director:
Tim Langenberg

Designer:
Tim Langenberg

Client:
Oklahoma Jazz Hall of Fame

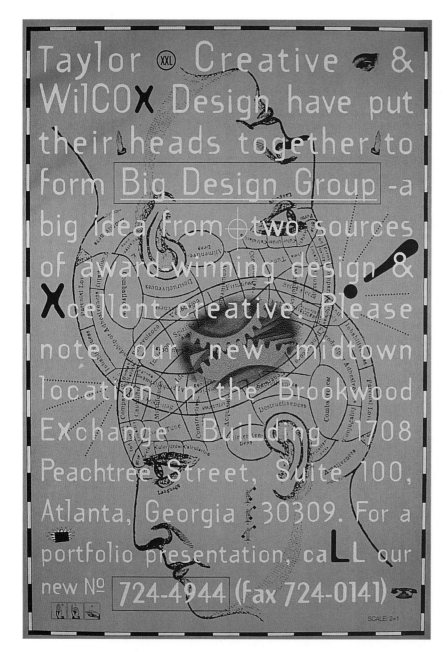

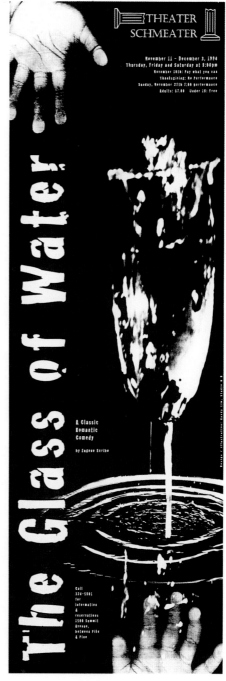

LEFT
Project:
Big Design Group Announcement

Design Firm:
Big Design Group

Art Director:
Michael Taylor

Designer:
Michael Taylor

Illustrator:
Michael Taylor

Photographer:
David Smith

Client:
Big Design Group

RIGHT
Project:
The Glass of Water Poster

Design Firm:
Studio M D

Art Directors:
Randy Lim, Jesse Doquilo,
Glenn Mitsui

Designer:
Randy Lim

Illustrator:
Randy Lim

Client:
Theater Schmeater

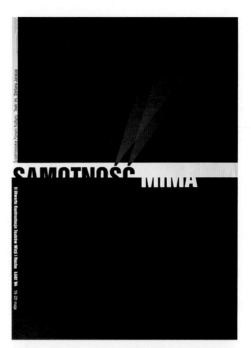

TOP LEFT
Project:
KUNSTHAUS Poster

Design Firm:
BBV Baviera

Art Director:
Michael Baviera

Designer:
Roger Steck

Photographer:
Jean Pierre Kuhn

Client:
Stiftung Für

BOTTOM LEFT
Project:
The Twilight Zone Poster

Design Firm:
Studio M D

Art Directors:
Randy Lim, Jesse Doquilo,
Glenn Mitsui

Designer:
Randy Lim

Illustrator:
Randy Lim

Client:
Theater Schmeater

TOP RIGHT
Project:
Mime's Solitude/
Samotnosc Mima Poster

Design Firm:
Atelier Tadeusz Piechura

Art Director:
Tadeusz Piechura

Designer:
Tadeusz Piechura

Client:
Srodmiejskie Forum Kultury

BOTTOM RIGHT
Project:
Brotherhood and Unity Poster

Design Firm:
Cedomir Kostovic

Art Director:
Cedomir Kostovic

Designer:
Cedomir Kostovic

Illustrator:
Cedomir Kostovic

Silkscreen Print:
Ken Daley

Client:
Art and Design Department
SMSU

Queuing up to show your work to Southern California's top graphic designers at the March 4 portfolio review might be a bit intimidating. Maybe you're not a graduating senior, grad student, or new graduate, but you still want to know more about portfolios. Come to Otis College of Art and Design on Saturday, February 5 at 9:00 a.m. for a morning of portfolio theory, helpful hints, hand-holding and just about whatever you need to get yourself ready for the big time. Bring your portfolio (or whatever you have that might turn into a portfolio) if you want particular advice, but it's not required. The day's free (except for parking, which is $3, so carpool) and open to recent graduates and all students. Talks, demonstrations, and miscellaneous tap-dancing start at 9:00 and go on until 12:00. Your department office will have schedules and a map.

PORTFOLIO?

A

The American Institute of Graphic Arts

is a

national non-profit organisation that promotes excellence in graphic design. Student membership is only $35 per year. Student members receive various publications including the "AIGA Journal," published quarterly, and the AIGA membership directory (one of the most useful tools for anyone looking for a job in graphic design). Information on AIGA/LA events and free admission to four of them.

"Propaganda," the Los Angeles Chapter newsletter, provides a calendar of events including speakers, discussions, and special programs for students and recent graduates like "small talks" on starting out in the design business and portfolio days. Both portfolio events are free to student members. (The portfolio preparation seminar at Otis is free to all students.)

You can find out about current AIGA/LA events by calling our information line at 310/364-1788. (It's a recording, so don't call to ask for directions if you're lost on the way to Otis.) For membership information call AIGA national at 800/548-1634 or White Design at 310/597-7772.

Be sure to find out about AIGA/LA's summer internship

Word cloud (left page): KEEP · PEACE · FRIEND · LIFE · SMILE · SUN · EARTH · CULTURE · LOVE · OCEAN · NATURE · JUSTICE · KEEP

graphic design student
PORTFOLIO
review

The Los Angeles chapter of the American Institute of Graphic Arts incorporating ADLA – the Art Directors Club of Los Angeles will host a portfolio review for graduating seniors and new graduates on Friday, March 31, 1995, at Pacific Design Center Blue Conference Center. Representatives of Southern California's best design firms will be on hand to look at your portfolio and give you advice.

Registration starts at 9:00 a.m. At 10:00 David Goodman will give a talk on finding a job. We'll take a break from 11:45 until 12:45. Portfolio showing will go from 1:00 p.m. until 4:00 p.m.

The cost is just $25 for the day. Better yet, spend $40 and become an AIGA member then the Portfolio Review is free. Parking at the PDC is $6.

Friday,
March 31, 1995

SPONSORS:
Alan Lithri
Homeyfee Inc.
Strathmore Paper
Westland Graphics
PATRONS:
Anderson Lithri
Andresen Graphic Services
Apple Computer
Bordjet, Inc.
Donahue Printing
Electric Pencil
George Rice & Sons
G.P. Color
Graphic Arts Center
House of Packaging
Icon West
Lettergraphics
Lithographix, Inc.
Micro Publishing News

The American Institute of Graphic Arts is a national non-profit organization that promote excellence in graphic design. Student membership is only $40 per year. Student members recieve various publications including the "AIGA Journal" and the Annual

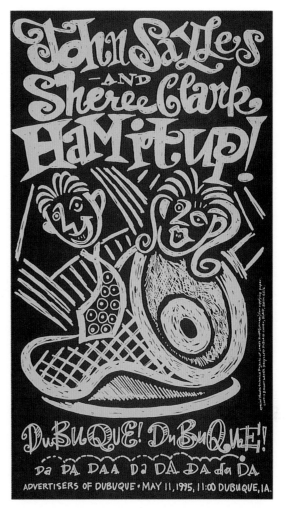

Project:
John Sayles and Sheree Clark
In Tune Poster

Project:
John Sayles and Sheree Clark
Ham It Up Poster

Design Firm:
Sayles Graphic Design

Design Firm:
Sayles Graphic Design

Art Director:
John Sayles

Art Director:
John Sayles

Designer:
John Sayles

Designer:
John Sayles

Illustrator:
John Sayles

Illustrator:
John Sayles

Client:
Cedar Rapids Advertising
Federation

Client:
Advertisers of Dubuque

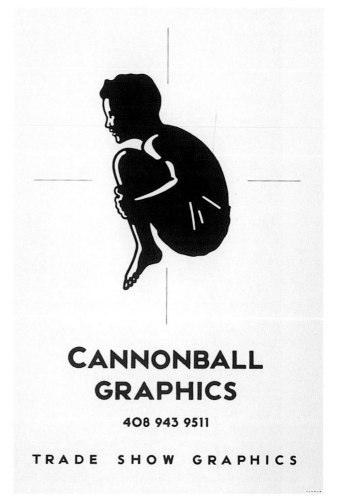

Project:
John Sayles and Sheree Clark
In High Gear Poster

Design Firm:
Sayles Graphic Design

Art Director:
John Sayles

Designer:
John Sayles

Illustrator:
John Sayles

Client:
AIGA/Detroit

Project:
Cannonball Graphics Poster

Design Firm:
Michael Schwab Design

Designer:
Michael Schwab

Illustrator:
Michael Schwab

Model:
Eric Schwab

Client:
Cannonball Graphics

Earth Day Northwest presents

EARTH DAY 25
25TH ANNIVERSARY

Saturday April 22
Events Regionwide

for events in your area
call 1 800 RECYCLE (M-F 8am-5pm)

Sunday April 23
Free Concert Celebration Pier 48
Pioneer Square

Seattle

Sponsored by: KSTW Northwest 11 • Puget Power • People for Puget Sound • Washington State Department of Ecology
Earth Day Northwest 1326 Fifth Ave., Suite 460 Seattle, WA 98101 (206) 343 7717
POSTER DESIGN: TIM GIRVIN DESIGN, INC.
PRINTED ON RECYCLED PAPER

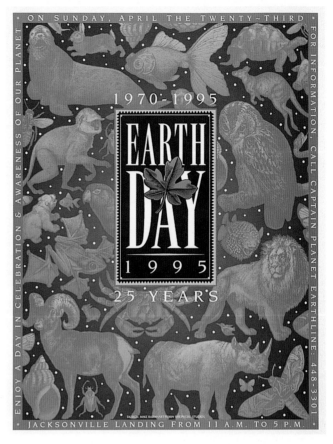

Project:
Earth Day Jacksonville
Celebration Poster

Project:
Earth Day Jacksonville
Celebration Animal Poster

Design Firm:
Robin Shepherd Studios

Design Firm:
Robin Shepherd Studios

Art Director:
Mike Barnhart

Art Director:
Mike Barnhart

Designer:
Mike Barnhart

Designer:
Mike Barnhart

Printer:
Financial Printing

Printer:
Fidelity Press

Client:
Earth Day Jacksonville Chapter

Client:
Earth Day Jacksonville Chapter

Project:
1993 AIGA/LA Student Portfolio
Events Poster

Design Firm:
Gunnar Swanson Design Office

Art Director:
Gunnar Swanson

Designer:
Gunnar Swanson

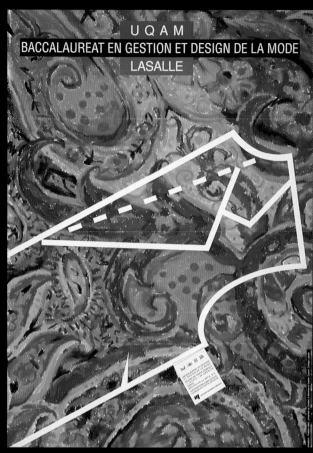

Project:
Fairview/Happy Chinese
New Year Poster

Design Firm:
2 Dimensions Inc.
Advertising by Design

Art Director:
Kam Wai Yu

Designers:
Kam Wai Yu, Mic Hung

Client:
Cad

Project:
Baccalauréat du Gestion et
Design de la Mode

Design Firm:
Bretelle-UQAM

Art Director:
Frédéric Metz

Designer:
Frédéric Metz

Illustrator:
Gaetan Gauvin

Client:
Ecole Supérieure de la

Project:
Rethink, Reduce, Reuse, Recycle Poster

Design Firm:
Hansen Design Company

Art Director:
Pat Hansen

Designers:
Pat Hansen, Kip Henrie

Illustrators:
Kip Henrie, Pat Hansen

Sponsor:
State of Washington Department
of Ecology

Client:
The G.A.P. (Growth and Prevention)
Theatre Company

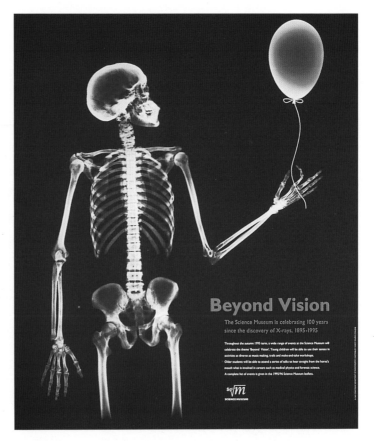

LEFT

Project:
HempFest Poster

Design Firm:
Art Chantry, Jamie Sheehan

Art Directors:
Art Chantry, Jamie Sheehan

Designers:
Art Chantry, Jamie Sheehan

Illustrators:
Art Chantry, Jamie Sheehan

Client:
Seattle Peace Heathens

RIGHT

Project:
Science Museum X-Ray Poster

Design Firm:
Lewis Moberly

Art Director:
Bryan Clark

Designer:
Robert Howsam

Photographer:
Department of Radiography,
Christ Church College

Client:
The Science Museum

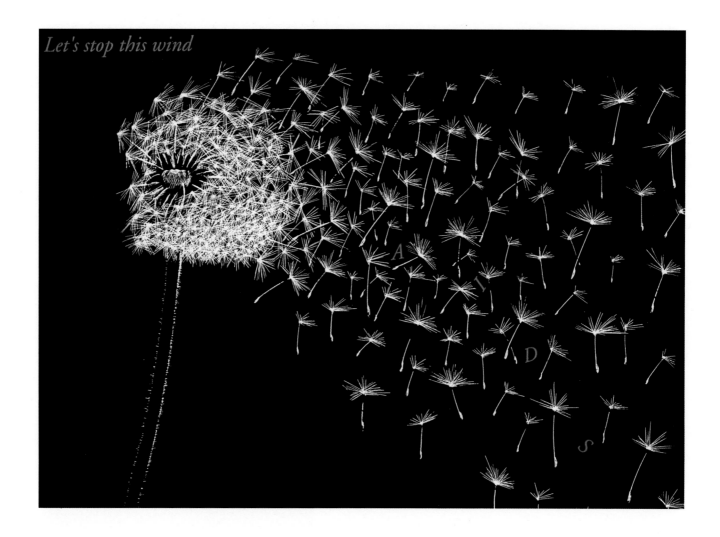

Let's stop this wind

Project:
Let's Stop this Wind—
AIDS Poster

Design Firm:
Cedomir Kostovic

Art Director:
Cedomir Kostovic

Designer:
Cedomir Kostovic

Illustrator:
Cedomir Kostovic

Silkscreen Print:
Ken Daley

Client:
Art and Design Department
SMSU

Project:
"Geld ist Nicht Alles..."/
"Money Isn't Everything..." Poster

Design Firm:
Karl Design

Art Director:
Andreas Karl

Designer:
Andreas Karl

Illustrator:
Andreas Karl

Client:
Afrika-Klub

Project:
AIDS Walk Poster

Design Firm:
Vaughn Wedeen Creative, Inc.

Art Director:
Steve Wedeen

Designer:
Steve Wedeen

Illustrator:
Vivian Harder

Computer Production:
Heather Scanlon

Client:
AIDS Services of New Mexico

Project:
Man In Danger/Czlowiek W
Zagrozeniu Poster

Design Firm:
Atelier Tadeusz Piechura

Art Director:
Tadeusz Piechura

Designer:
Tadeusz Piechura

Client:
LDK–Lodzki Dom Kultury

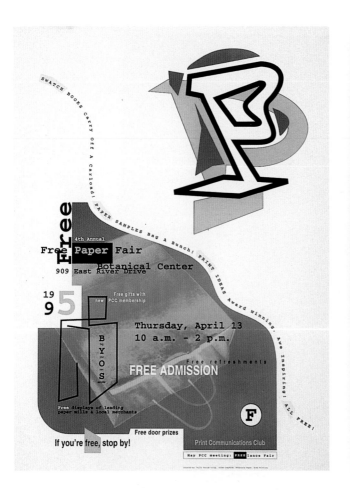

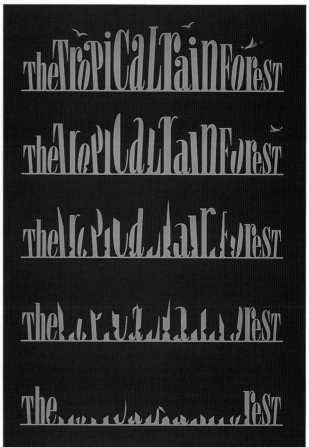

Project:
Print Communications Club
Paper Fair Poster

Design Firm:
CMF&Z Design

Art Director:
Brent Wirth

Designer:
Brent Wirth

Project Developer:
Janelle Allen

Copywriter:
Mark Lunde

Client:
Print Communications Club

Project:
The Tropical Rainforest Poster

Design Firm:
Karl Design

Art Director:
Andreas Karl

Designer:
Andreas Karl

Illustrator:
Andreas Karl

Client:
B.U.N.D., Bund Für Umwelt und
Naturschutz Deutschland

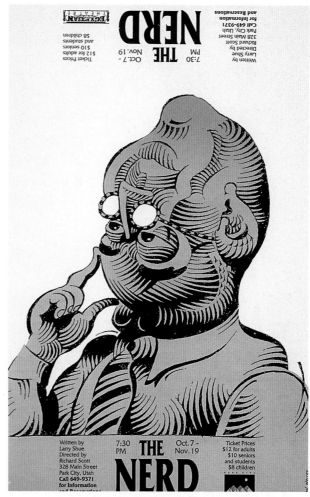

Project:
Ethnic Festival Poster

Design Firm:
Pitcock Design Group

Art Director:
Thomas Pitcock

Designers:
Thomas Pitcock, Scott Johnson

Illustrator:
Thomas Pitcock

Client:
City of South Bend, Indiana

Project:
The Nerd Poster

Design Firm:
The Weller Institute for the
Cure of Design, Inc.

Art Director:
Don Weller

Designer:
Don Weller

Illustrator:
Don Weller

Client:
Park City Performances

Project:
The Pricing Game Poster

Design Firm:
The Leonhardt Group

Designers:
Dennis Clouse, Traci Daberko,
Charlyne Fabi, Jeff Welsh,
Kaitlin Snyder

Illustrators:
Traci Daberko, Dennis Clouse

Client:
Graphic Artists Guild/Seattle

Project:
Festival Konda Lota Poster

Design Firm:
Kenzo Izutani Office Corporation

Art Director:
Kenzo Izutani

Designers:
Kenzo Izutani, Aki Hirai

Photographer:
Yasuyuki Amazutsumi

Client:
Conversation Company Ltd.

Project:
Springing The Blues Poster

Design Firm:
Robin Shepherd Studios

Art Directors:
Jefferson Rall, Robin Shepherd

Designer:
Jefferson Rall

Illustrator:
Jefferson Rall

Printer:
Cox Fine Art

Client:
Springing The Blues Festival

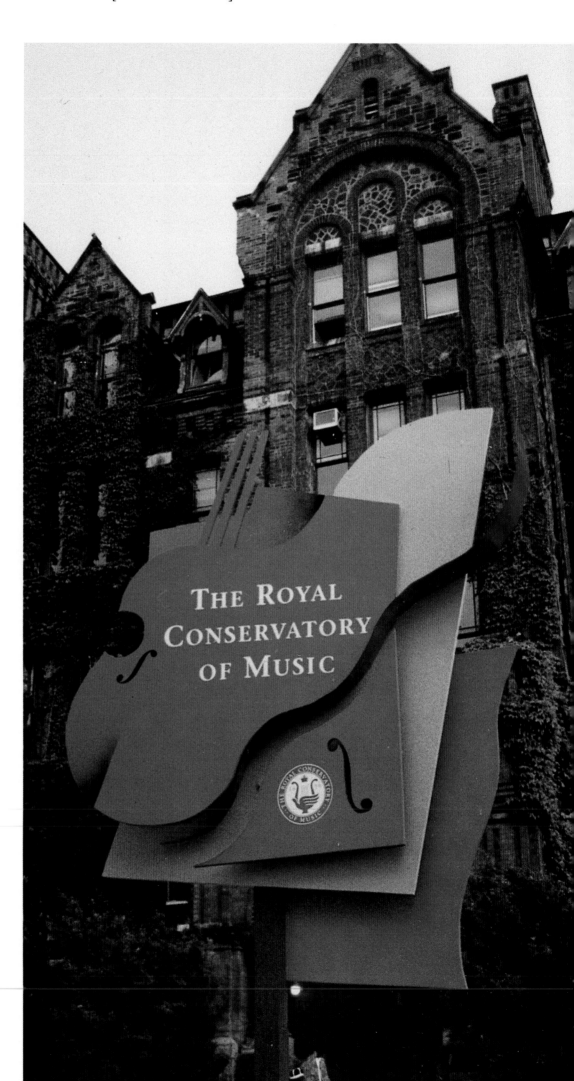

Project:
Exterior Identification Sign

Design Firm:
Janczak/Mandel Associates Inc.

Art Directors:
Carl Mandel, Voytek Janczak

Designers:
Carl Mandel, Voytek Janczak,
Rosanna Debenedictis

Client:
The Royal Conservatory of Music,
Toronto

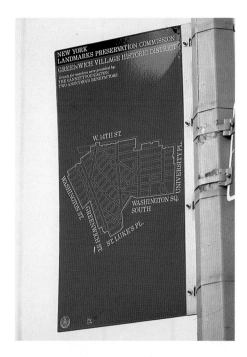
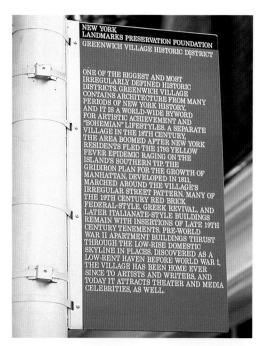

Project:
New York City Historical
District Markers and Street Signs

Design Firm:
Vignelli Associates

Art Director:
Massimo Vignelli

Designers:
Massimo Vignelli, Rebecca Rose

Photographer:
Luca Vignelli

Client:
New York Landmarks
Preservation Foundation

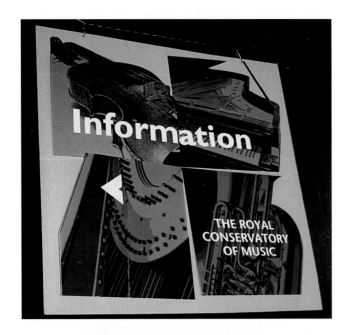

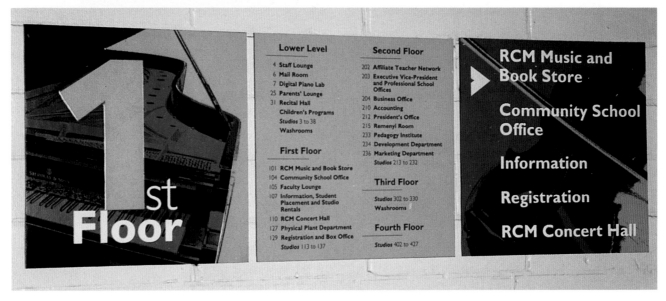

Project:
Interior Wayfinding
Signage System

Design Firm:
Janczak/Mandel Associates Inc.

Art Directors:
Voytek Janczak, Carl Mandel

Designers:
Voytek Janczak, Carl Mandel,
Rosanna Debenedictis

Photographer:
Voytek Janczak

Client:
The Royal Conservatory of
Music, Toronto

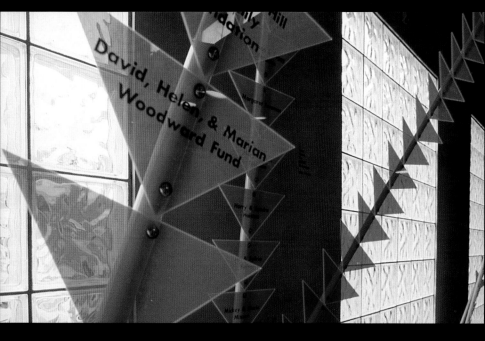

Project:
Nexus Contemporary Art Center–
Environmental Graphics

Design Firm:
Lorenc Design

Art Director:
Jan Lorenc

Designer:
Jan Lorenc

Illustrator:
Jan Lorenc

Photographer:
Jan Lorenc

Client:
Nexus–Louise Shaw

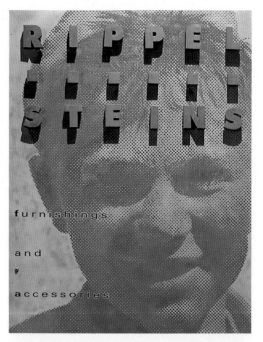

Project:
Chronicle Books/GiftWorks
Display

Design Firm:
Earl Gee Design

Art Director:
Earl Gee

Designer:
Earl Gee

Photographer:
Alan Shortall

Fabricator:
Barr Exhibits

Client:
Chronicle Books

TOP LEFT

Project:
Summer Hours Self-Promotion

Design Firm:
Design Horizons International

Designer:
Mike Schacherer

Client:
Design Horizons International

BOTTOM LEFT

Project:
Mimbres Pottery

Design Firm:
Pitcock Design Group

Art Director:
Thomas Pitcock

Designer:
Thomas Pitcock

Illustrator:
Thomas Pitcock

Copywriter:
Kathleen Desmond

Client:
Pitcock Design Group

TOP RIGHT

Project:
We Draw Circles Promotion

Design Firm:
Sayles Graphic Design

Art Director:
John Sayles

Designer:
John Sayles

Illustrator:
John Sayles

Client:
Sayles Graphic Design

BOTTOM RIGHT

Project:
White Design Holiday Cards

Design Firm:
White Design

Art Director:
John White

Designer:
Susan Foti

Illustrators:
Aram Youssefian, Susan Foti,
Carlos Delgado, Rick Olson,
Flatland, Jonathan Lun,
Roger Xavier

Photographer:
Russ Widstrand

Printer:
Costello Brothers

Client:
White Design

Project:
Conroy & Conroy Promotional
T-Shirt

Design Firm:
Conroy & Conroy

Art Director:
Maggie Conroy

Designer:
Sharon Wong

Illustrator:
Sharon Wong

Client:
Conroy & Conroy

Project:
Holiday Reserve Gift Package

Design Firm:
The Design Company

Art Directors:
Marcia Romanuck, Busha Husak

Designers:
Marcia Romanuck, Busha Husak

Illustrators:
Marcia Romanuck, Busha Husak

Photographer:
Marcia Romanuck

Client:
The Design Company

Project:
Take A Look Promotion

Design Firm:
Watson Creative Group

Art Director:
Dana Watson

Designer:
Mara Hines

Client:
Watson Creative Group

Print · Supon Design Group

Greg was thirteen when his parents gave him his

first recording of Aida for Christmas. For the next

three months, he listened to the entire opera

every day after he had finished his homework—

or sometimes instead of doing his homework.

Luckily for his parents, the recording wore out

eventually. Now he has over thirty recordings

of Aida. After he told us this story, he sat at

the keyboard and sang the entire opera—from

the overture to the part where the fat lady sings,

stage directing each scene as he went, including

the elephants. And I said, "Do it again!"

GREGORY FROESE, SINGER/PIANIST

Graphis · Supon Design Group · HOW · National Addy Creation

Overwhelming villains and divas dying at the top

of their lungs are too much for Dewin Tibbs. He has

a great big baritone voice and a personality to match.

When he takes the stage, he becomes the central

character. So I knew the work would somehow be

centered around a big bass clef. Then I thought of

him even as a singing figure. To my surprise, my first

sketch looked just like Dewin. When he saw the

mark, he was tickled to see a caricature of himself.

He thanked me for the trim waist and for including

some hair on top. Then he began laughing around the

room singing, "But you didn't give me any feet!"

DEWIN TIBBS, OPERATIC BARITONE

Project:
It's a Matter of Listening

Design Firm:
Komarow Design

Art Director:
Ronni Komarow

Designer:
Ronni Komarow

Illustrator:
Julia Talcott

Client:
Komarow Design

BOTTOM LEFT

Project:
White Design Holiday Chocolates
Promotion

Design Firm:
White Design

Art Director:
John White

Designer:
Aram Youssefian

Client:
White Design

TOP RIGHT

Project:
Poster Show by Kan Tai-keung

Design Firm:
Kan Tai-keung Design &
Associates Ltd

Art Director:
Kan Tai-keung

Designers:
Kan Tai-keung, Benjamin Wong
Wai Bun

Photographer:
C.K. Wong

Client:
The Artland Co. Ltd,
Artland Gallery

BOTTOM RIGHT

Project:
Marketing Mug

Design Firm:
Woods + Woods

Art Director:
Paul Woods

Designer:
Paul Woods

Illustrator:
Paul Woods

Client:
Woods + Woods

Project:
Season's Eatings Client Holiday Gift

Design Firm:
Lambert Design Studio

Art Director:
Christie Lambert

Designers:
Joy Cathey Price, Christie Lambert

Illustrator:
Joy Cathey Price

Photographer:
Richard Reens

Copywriter:
Scott Price

Client:
Lambert Design Studio

Project:
Amedeo/Photographers'
Self-Promotion

Design Firm:
BRD Design

Art Director:
Peter King Robbins

Designer:
Peter King Robbins

Photographer:
Amedeo

Client:
Amedeo

Project:
Ecological Card

Design Firm:
Mário Aurélio & Associados

Art Director:
Mário Aurélio

Designers:
Mário Aurélio, Rosa Maia

Photographer:
In Press/José Emidio

Client:
Mário Aurélio & Associados

graphic design
.corporate **identity** .direct mail .catalogs .packaging .book design .posters

[print & electronic media]

industrial design

2d+3d requirements are as much an effect of our lifestyles as they may be rudiments of ever... —we question the premise that form follows function— As we see again and again, if it is ... then there is little separation 'tween form & function as it occurs in succes...

[whatever it is]*

call it what you will
*product or service
when is it that it is not
communication?

how can we convince others of something
of absolute belief to ourselves,
if we are not able to share that often small,
intrinsic quality that rests at the base
of the thing we believe?

graef + ziller design
330 fell street, san francisco...

Project:
Graef & Ziller Design Promotion

Design Firm:
Graef & Ziller Design

Art Directors:
Barbara Ziller, Andrew Graef

Designers:
Andrew Graef, Barbara Ziller

Illustrator:
Elaine Hodges—Smithsonian (bees)

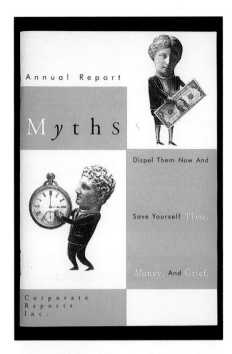

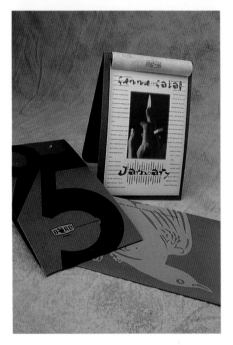

Project:
Annual Report Myths

Design Firm:
Corporate Reports Inc.

Art Director:
Brant Day

Designer:
Brant Day

Illustrator:
Brant Day

Copywriter:
Sandra Dempsey Furbish

Client:
Corporate Reports Inc.

Project:
Self-Promotion Calendar

Design Firm:
BRD Design

Art Director:
Peter King Robbins

Designer:
Peter King Robbins

Illustrator:
David Goldin

Photographers:
Amedeo, Glen Erler,
Jeremy Samuelson, Stuart Watson,
Catherine Ledner, Philip Salaverry

Copywriter:
Barry Yourgrau

Client:
BRD Design

Project:
Year-End Card

Design Firm:
Dookim Design

Art Director:
Doo H. Kim

Designers:
Dongil Lee, Seunghee Lee

Client:
Dookim Design

Project:
CD Case Self-Promotion

Design Firm:
Kirk Miller & John Klein

Art Directors:
Kirk Miller & John Klein

Designers:
Kirk Miller & John Klein

Client:
Kirk Miller & John Klein

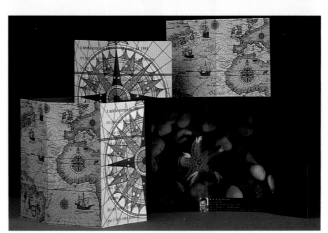

TOP LEFT

Project:
Hornall Anderson Design Works
Holiday Card

Design Firm:
Hornall Anderson Design Works, Inc.

Art Director:
Jack Anderson

Designers:
Jack Anderson, Mary Hermes

Client:
Hornall Anderson Design Works, Inc.

BOTTOM LEFT

Project:
Nigel Parry Calling Card

Design Firm:
Pentagram Design Limited

Art Director:
Justus Oehler

Designer:
Justus Oehler

Photographer:
Nigel Parry

Client:
Nigel Parry

TOP RIGHT

Project:
Company Christmas Card

Design Firm:
Wang & Williams

Art Director:
Ming Wang

Designers:
Ming Wang, Denise Williams

Illustrator:
Ming Wang

Client:
Wang & Williams

BOTTOM RIGHT

Project:
The Star Of My Sea

Design Firm:
Mário Aurélio & Associados

Art Director:
Mário Aurélio

Designers:
Mário Aurélio, Rosa Maia

Photographer:
In Press/José Emidio

Client:
Mário Aurélio & Associados

TOP

Project:

T.P. Postcard Series

Design Firm:

CENTER

Project:

A Book of Marks Self-Promotion

Designer:

BOTTOM

Project:

BRD Design Self-Promoti

Design Firm:

Project:
Takigawa Design Notecards

Design Firm:
Jerry Takigawa Design

Art Director:
Jerry Takigawa

Designers:
Jerry Takigawa,
Glenn Johnson

Photographer:
Jerry Takigawa

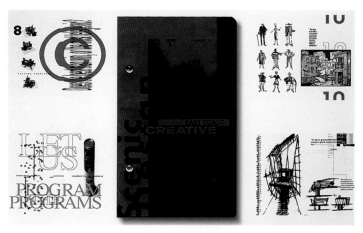

TOP	CENTER	BOTTOM
Project:	**Project:**	**Project:**
Pamplet TV #8	Shoes	Ott Shots Photo Book
Design Firm:	**Design Firm:**	**Design Firm:**
East Coast Creative	Resolute Communications Design	Dennard Creative, Inc.
Art Director:	**Art Director:**	**Art Director:**
Holland Wilde	Kathryn Kazunas	Bob Dennard
Designer:	**Designer:**	**Designer:**
Arthur Perry	Kathryn Kazunas	James Lacey
Client:	**Copywriter:**	**Photographer:**
East Coast Creative	Kathryn Kazunas	Jeff Ott
	Client:	**Client:**
	Resolute Communications Design	Jeff Ott Photography

Have a Heart

[A Valentine's Day Quiz]

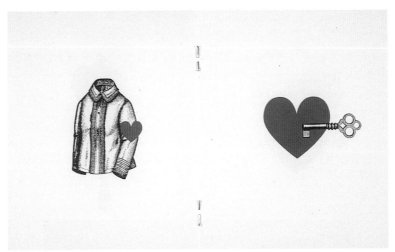

TOP AND CENTER

Project:
Valentine Card

Design Firm:
Toni Schowalter Design

Art Director:
Toni Schowalter

Designer:
Toni Schowalter

Client:
Toni Schowalter Design

BOTTOM

Project:
ISDN Promotion

Design Firm:
Corporate Reports Inc.

Art Director:
Brant Day

Designer:
Brant Day

Illustrator:
Brant Day

Copywriter:
Tim Hogan

Client:
Corporate Reports Inc.

have used? Did it focus on the negatives and ignore the positives? Only through direct communication can you make sure the right and total message is getting through loud and clear.

3. The quarterly report becomes a part of your permanent record. Thorough quarterly reports, along with the annual report, provide a comprehensive historical record of your company's performance. They document continuity and consistency. For example, what happens when a company with a December year-end gets a request for information in November? With quarterly reports, you can fill that request with complete information – last year's annual and a set of quarterly reports.

4. It's only fair that all classes of stakeholders – individuals and institutions – have access to the same information. A complete, comprehensive quarterly report to all shareholders ensures that investors are treated fairly and that not just "the big boys" get the scoop.

shareholders own the company and deserve to be kept apprised of the performance, strategies and future direction their company is pursuing

make the most of your stamp

A poor communications vehicle – even when mailed as efficiently as possible – is still a waste of time and money. While you are taking a hard look at your postage bill, also consider taking a fresh approach to the quarterly itself.

- *all the news that fits.* Consider expanding the content of your quarterly report. It costs basically the same to send the standard tri-fold as it does an information-packed newsletter. The traditional quarterly report – a standard letter and statements – is somewhat informative but hardly enticing. Since you're buying the stamp anyway, send something that works harder for you. Include some operational highlights, significant events, product information, feature stories. Give your investors a reason to get excited about the company's future.

- *having a wonderful time; wish you were here.* Consider a postcard format for your quarterly report to shareholders. The Postal Service imposes size restrictions, but they give you a break on the postage. In this format, you can provide a brief, but meaningful, note from the CEO, financial highlights and significant events of the quarter. It's simple, fast, inexpensive. We'll show you how it works.

for pennies per copy, you give investors direct, unfiltered exposure to management's views and strategic direction

Project:
Quarterly Report Myths

Design Firm:
Corporate Reports Inc.

Art Director:
Brant Day

Designer:
Brant Day

Illustrator:
Brant Day

Copywriter:
Tim Hogan

Client:
Corporate Reports Inc.

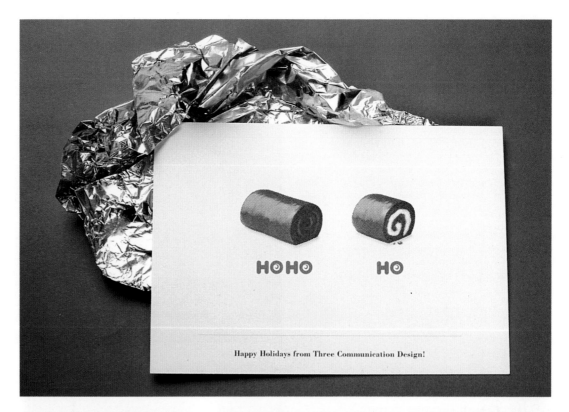

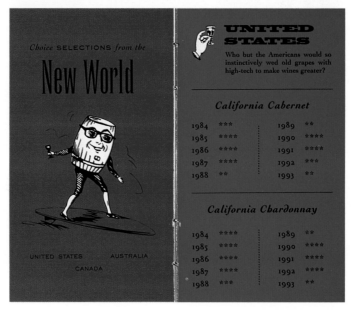

TOP

Project:
Holiday Card

Design Firm:
Three Communication Design

Designers:
Glenn Deutsch, Tony Porto,
Mitchell Rice

Client:
Three Communication Design

BOTTOM

Project:
Christmas Wine Guide Promotion

Design Firm:
Campbell Sheffield Design

Art Director:
Paul Campbell

Designers:
Paul Campbell, Greg Stevenson

Illustrator:
Paul Campbell

Client:
Campbell Sheffield Design

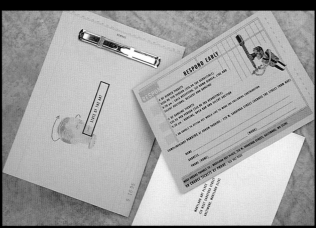

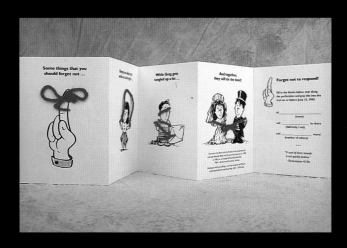

TOP

Project:
Fall Presentation Party Invitation

Design Firm:
WLVI-TV 56

Art Director:
Cheryl Greatorex

Designer:
Cheryl Greatorex

Illustrator:
Cheryl Greatorex

Client:
WLVI-TV 56

CENTER

Project:
Maryland Art Place Benefit
Exhibition & Auction

Design Firm:
GKV Design

Art Director:
Gene Valle

Designer:
Gene Valle

Illustrator:
David Plunkert

Client:
Maryland Art Place

BOTTOM

Project:
Forget Not Invitation

Design Firm:
Firehouse Graphics

Art Director:
Mark Chez

Designer:
Mark Chez

Illustrator:
Mark Chez

Client:
Greg Fraser, Betty De

Project:
Breithaupt Invitation

Design Firm:
Sheehan Design

Art Director:
Jamie Sheehan

Designer:
Jamie Sheehan

Illustrator:
Jamie Sheehan

Copywriter:
Jamie Sheehan

Printer:
Thingmaker

Client:
Michele
Niewiadomski

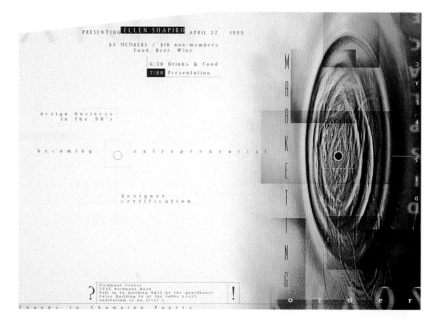

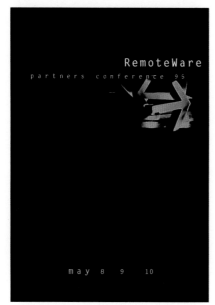

TOP
Project:
AIGA Atlanta/Ellen Shapiro

Design Firm:
Melia Design Group

Art Director:
Jordan Patsios

Designers:
Jordan Patsios, Roth Ritter

Client:
AIGA Atlanta

BOTTOM
Project:
Remoteware Partners Invitation

Design Firm:
Melia Design Group

Art Director:
D.T. Teeslink

Designer:
Todd Simmons

Photographer:
Sonny Williams

Client:
Xcellenet

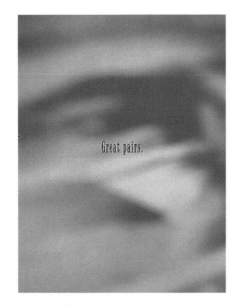

Great pairs.

Confident of their lasting love,

the twosome startled friends and family

with unsettling shows of sweetness.

It was more than infatuation, it was a

devotion most refined and rich.

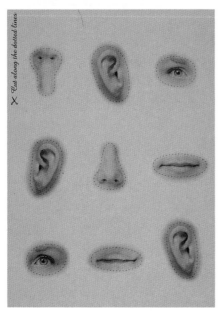

Cut along the dotted lines

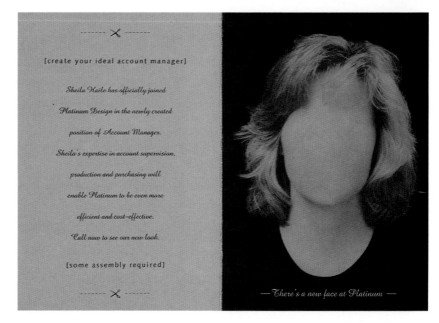

[create your ideal account manager]

Sheila Haile has officially joined
Platinum Design in the newly created
position of Account Manager.
Sheila's expertise in account supervision,
production and purchasing will
enable Platinum to be even more
efficient and cost-effective.
Call now to see our new look.

[some assembly required]

—There's a new face at Platinum—

TOP
Project:
Fedell Wedding/
Bachelor Party Invitations

Design Firm:
After Hours Creative

Art Director:
After Hours Creative

Designer:
After Hours Creative

Illustrator:
After Hours Creative

Photographer:
Tim Lanterman

Client:
Tiffany Fedell

BOTTOM
Project:
A New Face Announcement

Design Firm:
Platinum Design, Inc.

Art Director:
Kathleen Phelps

Designers:
Kathleen Phelps, Kelly Hogg

Photographer:
Paul Lachenaur

Client:
Platinum Design

Project:
The Schottenstein Dormitory
Dedication Invitation

Design Firm:
The Columbus College of
Art & Design

Art Director:
John Kirk

Designer:
John Kirk

Photographer:
Duncan Snyder

Client:
The Columbus College of
Art & Design

Project:
Fish BBQ T-Shirt

Design Firm:
After Hours Creative

Art Director:
After Hours Creative

Designer:
After Hours Creative

Illustrator:
After Hours Creative

Client:
Phoenix Chapter of AIGA

J&J

Jeff and Jenae Miller
are pleased to announce the most recent
addition to their family

j

Jane Madison Miller
Born February 4, 1995
4 lbs. 14 oz., 17 3/4 inches

TOP
Project:
Regal Name Change Party
Invitation

Design Firm:
Dennard Creative, Inc.

Art Director:
Bob Dennard

Designers:
Bob Dennard, Wayne Geyer

Illustrator:
Chris Wood

Client:
Regal Printing

BOTTOM
Project:
Birth Announcement

Design Firm:
Corsetti Design

Art Director:
Shawn R. Hansen

Designer:
Shawn R. Hansen

Client:
Jenaé Miller

Project:
Regal Name Change Party
Invitation

Design Firm:
Dennard Creative, Inc.

Art Director:
Bob Dennard

Designers:
Bob Dennard, Wayne Geyer

Illustrator:
Chris Wood

Client:
Regal Printing

Project:
Save The Woodlands Campaign

Design Firm:
Parham Santana Design Inc.

Creative Directors:
Maruchi Santana, Rick Tesoro

Designers:
Jeanne Greco, Randy Zwirn

Client:
Prospect Park Alliance

Please do not attend.

Stay away.

We'd really rather not see you.

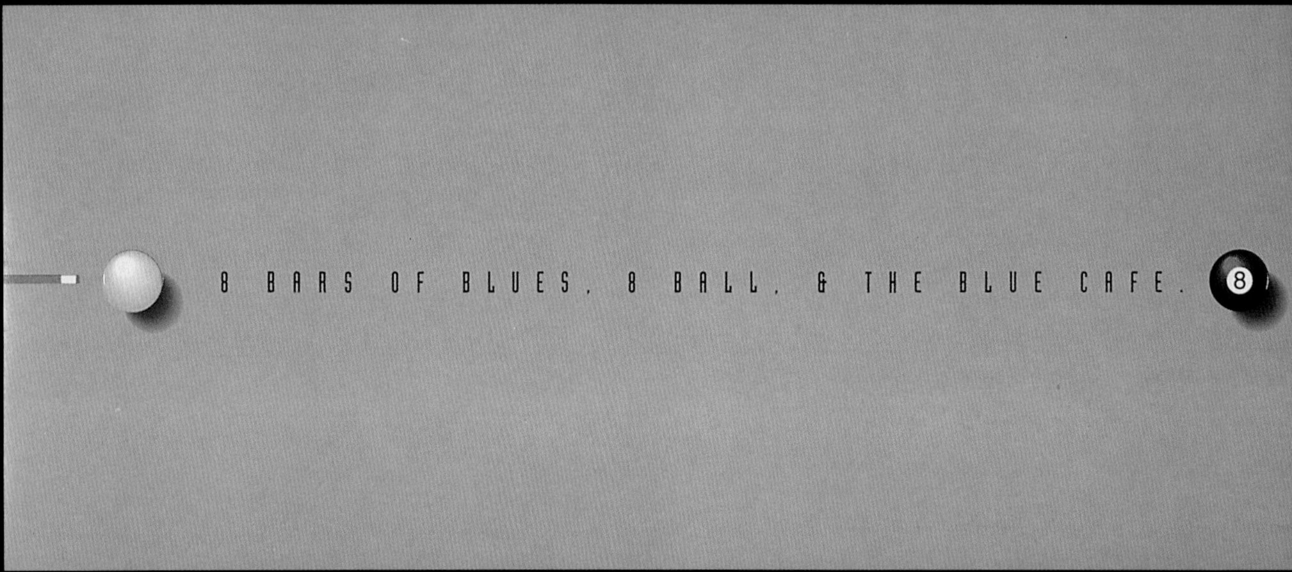

8 BARS OF BLUES, 8 BALL, & THE BLUE CAFE. 8

TOP

Project:
Stay Away Party Invitation

Design Firm:
After Hours Creative

BOTTOM

Project:
8 Bars of Blue Invitation

Design Firm:
Jensen Design Associates

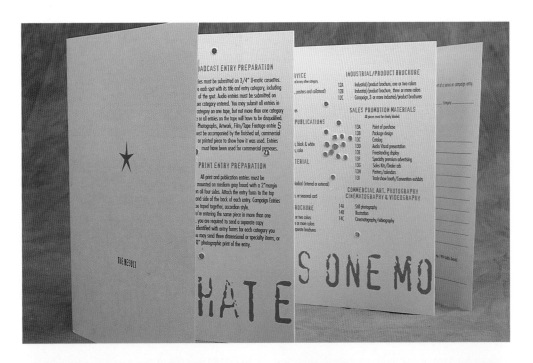

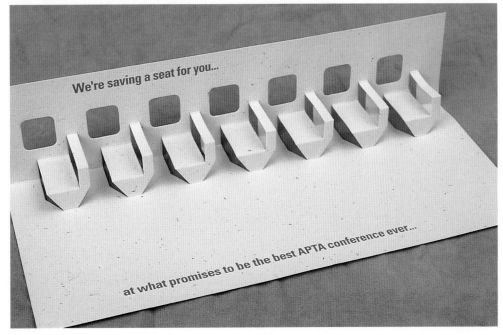

We're saving a seat for you...

at what promises to be the best APTA conference ever...

TOP

Project:
Addy Awards Call for Entries

Design Firm:
After Hours Creative

Art Director:
After Hours Creative

Designer:
After Hours Creative

Printing and Drilling:
Heritage Graphics

Client:
Phoenix Ad Club

BOTTOM

Project:
Moving Toward Tomorrow
Conference Invitation

Design Firm:
Sexton Design

Art Director:
Randall Sexton

Designers:
Randall Sexton, Eddie Yuen

Copywriter:
Scott Leeper

Client:
Transportation Agency,
Santa Clara County

JOIN US

[A T H E N S]

[N E E N A M]

Come in, We're
OPEN

ANN'S
GRILL

[ATHENS PAPER]

AND

[NEENAH]

INVITE YOU

TO HAVE LUNCH

WITH US

AT

VINCENZO'S

TUESDAY, AUGUST 9, 1994

FROM

11:45 AM — 1:00 PM

RSVP

BY FRIDAY, AUGUST 5, 1994

KRIS MILLER

361 2800

TOP RIGHT

Project:
World Cup Soccer Stamp:
First Day Issue Invitation

Design Firm:
Supon Design Group

Project Director:
Terrence McCaffrey

Art Director:
Supon Phornirunlit

Designer:
Apisak "Eddie" Saibua

Illustrator:
Apisak "Eddie" Saibua

Client:
U.S. Postal Service

BOTTOM RIGHT

Project:
Wonders of the Sea Stamp:
First Day Issue Invitation

Design Firm:
Supon Design Group

Project Director:
Terrence McCaffrey

Art Director:
Supon Phornirunlit

Designer:
Anthony Michael Fletcher

Client:
U.S. Postal Service

TOP LEFT

Project:
Net Information Systems
Direct Mail Piece

Design Firm:
The Leonhardt Group

Designers:
Jeff Welsh, Jon Cannell

Client:
Net Information Systems, Inc.

BOTTOM LEFT

Project:
Christmas Postcard

Design Firm:
Mário Aurélio & Associados

Art Director:
Mário Aurélio

Designers:
Mário Aurélio, Rosa Maia

Client:
Nove de Julho Printing

Project:
E=mc²

Design Firm:
Firehouse Graphics

Art Director:
Mark Chez

Designer:
Mark Chez

Photographer:
Blake Martin

Client:
Mark Chez, Michelle Chan

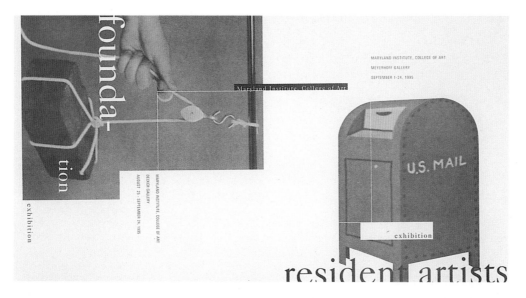

TOP
Project:
Maryland Institute, College of Art
Exhibition Cards

Design Firm:
Kurt Thesing, Gene Valle

Art Directors:
Kurt Thesing, Gene Valle

Designers:
Kurt Thesing, Gene Valle

Client:
Maryland Institute, College of Art

BOTTOM LEFT
Project:
Moving Announcement

Design Firm:
Telmet Design Associates

Designer:
Tiit Telmet

Printer:
C.J. Graphics Inc.

Client:
Telmet Design Associates

BOTTOM CENTER
Project:
Pittsburgh X 7 Exhibition
Announcement

Design Firm:
Sheirer Graphic Design

Art Director:
Lisa L. Sheirer

Designer:
Lisa L. Sheirer

Illustrator:
Lisa L. Sheirer

Photographer:
Lisa L. Sheirer

Client:
Stephanie Ann Roper Gallery,
Department of Visual Arts,
Frostburg State University

BOTTOM RIGHT
Project:
One Party Invitation

Design Firm:
Shelby Designs & Illustrates

Designer:
Shelby Putnam Tupper

Photographer:
Daniel David

Client:
Shelby Designs & Illustrates

Project:
Winterhalter/Goldfoot
Wedding Invitation

Design Firm:
Boom Design

Art Director:
Larissa Winterhalter

Designers:
Larissa Winterhalter, Joel Goldfoot

Photographer:
Larissa Winterhalter

Client:
Larissa Winterhalter, Joel Goldfoot

TOP
Project:
Sink or Swim Party Invitation

Design Firm:
Lambert Design Studio

Art Director:
Christie Lambert

Designer:
Joy Cathey Price

Illustrator:
Joy Cathey Price

Photographer:
Richard Reens

Client:
Lambert Design Studio

BOTTOM
Project:
American Center in Paris
Announcements and Calendar

Design Firm:
Vignelli Associates

Art Director:
Massimo Vignelli

Designers:
Massimo Vignelli, Rebecca Rose,
Chris DiMaggio

Photographer:
Luca Vignelli

Client:
American Center in Paris

TOP

Project:
Markoff Wedding Invitation

Design Firm:
London Road Design

Art Director:
Jan Haseman

Designer:
Martin Haseman

Printer:
Julie Holcomb

Client:
Leslie Markoff

BOTTOM

Project:
AIGA Design Camp Confirmation Postcard

Design Firm:
AIGA/Seattle Design Camp
Design Committee

Art Director:
Pat Hansen

Designers:
Pat Hansen, Kip Henrie,
Michael Conners, Kirk Stanford

Images:
Bruce Forster, Charles Mauzy

Printer:
Grossberg Tyler

Client:
AIGA/Seattle

TOP LEFT

Project:
Marilyn Monroe Stamp:
First Day Issue Invitation

Design Firm:
Supon Design Group

Project Director:
Terrence McCaffrey

Art Directors:
Andrew Dolan, Andrew Berman

Designer:
Mimi Eanes

Photographs:
UPI/Bettmann (cover),
The Kobal Collection Ltd. (inside)

Client:
U.S. Postal Service
(Marilyn Monroe name, image, and likeness
property of The Estate of Marilyn Monroe)

TOP RIGHT

Project:
Fultz Design Group
Open House Invitation

Design Firm:
CMF&Z Design

Art Director:
Brent Wirth

Designer:
Brent Wirth

Copywriters:
Pat Fultz, Mark Lunde

Client:
Fultz Design Group
(now CMF&Z Design)

BOTTOM

Project:
Norman Rockwell Stamp:
First Day Issue Invitation

Design Firm:
Supon Design Group

Project Director:
Terrence McCaffrey

Art Director:
Supon Phornirunlit

Designer:
Debbi Savitt

Client:
U.S. Postal Service

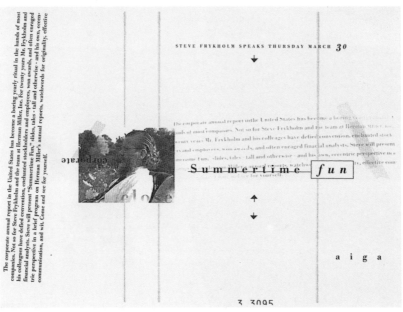

TOP
Project:
We've Moved to the Beach
Announcement

Design Firm:
Kirk Miller

Art Director:
Kirk Miller

Designer:
Kirk Miller

Silkscreen:
Gordon Silkscreen

Client:
Kirk Miller

BOTTOM
Project:
AIGA Atlanta/Steve Frykholm

Design Firm:
Melia Design Group

Art Director:
Todd Simmons

Designer:
Todd Simmons

Client:
AIGA Atlanta

Project:
Wedding Invitation

Design Firm:
Wöhlnick Design

Art Director:
Karel Wöhlnick

Designer:
Karel Wöhlnick

Client:
Teresa Fernandez

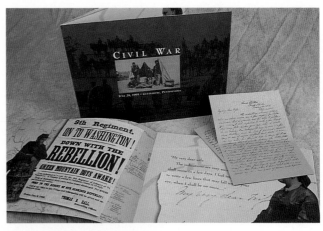

Project:
"Boldly Into Tomorrow"
Campaign Invitation

Design Firm:
Hornall Anderson
Design Works, Inc.

Art Director:
Jack Anderson

Designers:
Jack Anderson, Jani Drewfs, Cliff
Chung, Brian O'Neill, David Bates

Illustrators:
David Bates, Brian O'Neill

Client:
Food Services of America

Project:
Manes Space: Changes
Announcement

Design Firm:
Toni Schowalter Design

Art Director:
Toni Schowalter

Designer:
Toni Schowalter

Client:
Manes Space

Project:
Civil War Stamp:
First Day Issue Invitation

Design Firm:
Supon Design Group

Project Director:
Terrence McCaffrey

Art Directors:
Supon Phornironlit, Andy Dolan

Designer:
Mike LaManna

Client:
U.S. Postal Service

Project:
Conroy + Conroy Moving
Announcement

Design Firm:
Conroy + Conroy

Art Director:
Maggie Conroy

Designer:
Sharon Wong

Illustrator:
Sharon Wong

Copywriter:
Casey Conroy

Client:
Conroy + Conroy

Project:
A Taste of Chocolate Invitation

Design Firm:
Jon Wells Associates

Art Director:
Jon Wells

Designer:
Jon Wells

Client:
East Bay Habitat for Humanity

Project:
MLR Holiday Card,
Ornament, and Wrap

Designer:
Michele Rayome

Client:
Michele Rayome

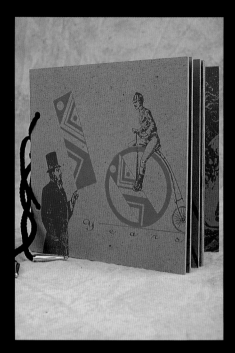

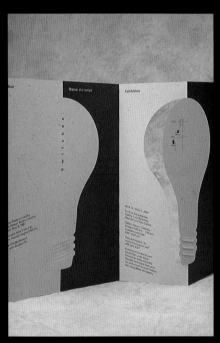

TOP LEFT

Project:
Vaughn Wedeen 10th Anniversary
Announcement

Design Firm:
Vaughn Wedeen Creative

Art Directors:
Rick Vaughn, Steve Wedeen

Designer:
Rick Vaughn

Illustrator:
Rick Vaughn

Mechanical:
Stan McCoy

BOTTOM LEFT

Project:
Platinum Record Announcement

Design Firm:
Platinum Design Inc.

Art Director:
Kathleen Phelps

Designer:
Kathleen Phelps

Client:
Platinum Design

TOP RIGHT

Project:
Jazz Instrumentalists Stamp:
First Day Issue Invitation

Design Firm:
Supon Design Group

Project Director:
Terrence McCaffrey

Art Director:
Supon Phornirunlit

Designer:
Debbi Savitt

Client:
U.S. Postal Service

BOTTOM RIGHT

Project:
Switches, Art Lamps
Auction/Exhibit

Design Firm:
Sexton Design

Art Director:
Randall Sexton

Designers:
Randall Sexton, Louis Chan

Client:
San Jose State University School
of Art and Design Alumni

Project:
Habitat for Humanity
Pavilion/Arts Festival of Atlanta

Design Firm:
Lorenc Design

Art Director:
Jan Lorenc

Designers:
Jan Lorenc, Sara Adkins

Photographers:
Rion Rizzo, Creative Sources
Photography

Fabricators:
Ken McGraw, Dan Reynolds

Client:
Habitat for Humanity/
Atlanta Chapter

Project:
Events Kit

Design Firm:
Spatchurst Design Associates

Art Director:
John Spatchurst

Designer:
Meryl Blundell

Client:
Gardner Merchant Australia

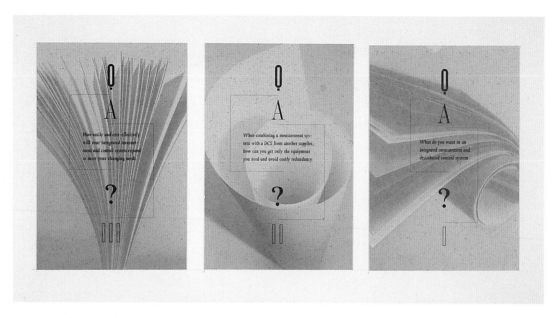

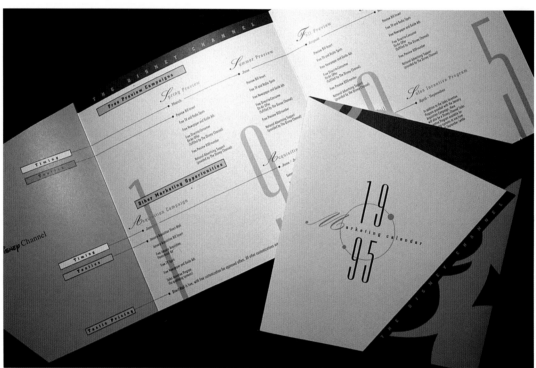

Project:
Impact Systems Direct Mail
Campaign

Design Firm:
Brad Terres Design

Art Director:
Brad Terres

Designer:
Brad Terres

Photographer:
Alan Blaustein

Client:
Impact Systems

Project:
Disney Channel Marketing
Calendar

Design Firm:
Vince Rini Design

Art Director:
Vince Rini

Designer:
Vince Rini

Client:
The Disney Channel

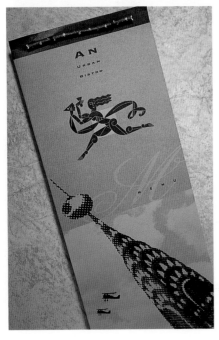

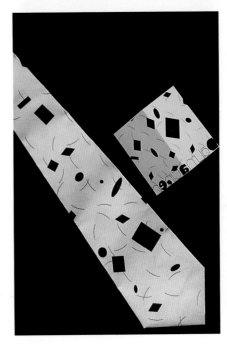

TOP LEFT

Project:
Anzu Menus

Design Firm:
David Carter Design

Art Director:
Sharon Lejeune

Creative Director:
Lori B. Wilson

Designer:
Sharon Lejeune

Illustrator:
Sharon Lejeune

Photographer:
Klein & Wilson Photography

Client:
Anzu

BOTTOM LEFT

Project:
Metropolitan Pizza Bar Menu

Design Firm:
Wilcox Design

Art Director:
Mark Wilcox

Designer:
Mark Wilcox

Illustrator:
Mark Wilcox

Client:
The Derek/Lawford Company

TOP RIGHT

Project:
Asia Pacific Copyright
Conference Pack

Design Firm:
Office B

Art Director:
Jacqui Bundy

Designer:
Jacqui Bundy

Illustrator:
Dover Illustration

Client:
Copyright Agency Limited

BOTTOM RIGHT

Project:
Croatia/Dalmatiner Tie

Design Firm:
Boris Ljubicic

Art Director:
Boris Ljubicic

Designer:
Boris Ljubicic

Illustrator:
Boris Ljubicic

Photographer:
Boris Ljubicic

Client:
Croata d.o.o.

Project:
TKO Logo/Symbol

Design Firm:
Asprey Di Donato Design

Art Director:
Peter Asprey

Designer:
Peter Asprey

Client:
The Ken Oath Theatre Co.

Project:
Ortho's Garden Planner

Design Firm:
Graef & Ziller Design

Art Director:
Barbara Ziller

Designers:
Barbara Ziller, Andrew Graef

Illustrator:
Cyndie C.H. Wooley
(black-and-white illustrations)

Photographers:
Kevin Sanchez, Andrew Graef,
Tony Stromberg, Josephine
Coatsworth, Michael McKinley,
James K. McNair, Michael Landis,
Michael Richards, Jack Napton,
Clyde Childress, Susan Lammers,
Barbara Ziller

Client:
Ortho Books

TOP

Project:
The Rain Forest Cafe
Catering Menu

Design Firm:
The Leonhardt Group

Designer:
Dennis Clouse

Client:
Woodland Park Zoological Society

BOTTOM

Project:
United Way Donor Kit

Design Firm:
Hornall Anderson Design Works, Inc.

Art Director:
John Hornall

Designers:
John Hornall, Jana Nishi,
The Leonhardt Group

Client:
United Way

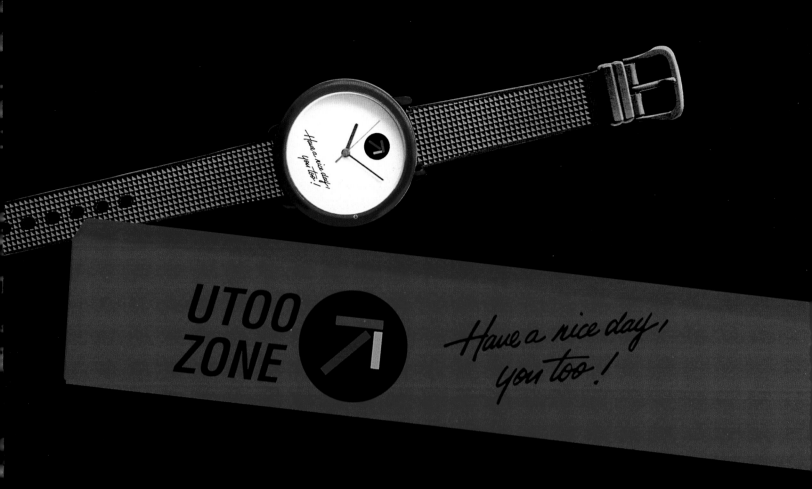

Project:
Utoo Zone–Samsung Corp. Watch

Design Firm:
Dookim Design

Art Director:
Doo H. Kim

Designers:
Dongil Lee, Seunghee Lee,
Jae Kyung Kwon

Agency:
Cheil Communications-CI Team

Client:
Samsung Corp–Utoo Zone

John Kirk
5633 Oslo Dr.
Westerville, OH 43081 U.S.A.
PAGE 22

Jon Wells Associates
407 Jackson St., #206
San Francisco, CA 94111 U.S.A.
PAGE 165

Joseph Gault & Associates
c/o 398 Adelaide Street West
Toronto, ON M5V 1S7 Canada
PAGE 93

Kan Tai-keung Design
& Associates Ltd
28/F Great Smart Tower
230 Wanchai Road
Hong Kong
PAGE 132

Karl Design
Rotlintstrasse 3
Frankfurt D-60316 Germany
PAGES 97, 116, 118

Kenzo Izutani Office Corporation
1-24-19 Fukasawa
Setagaya-ku, Tokyo 158 Japan
PAGES 81, 105, 121

Kirk Miller
4221 4th Ave.
San Diego, CA 92103 U.S.A.
PAGES 7, 162

Kirk Miller & John Klein
4221 4th Ave.
San Diego, CA 92103 U.S.A.
PAGE 135

Kleiner & Bold
Ostertorsteinweg 70/71
Bremen 28203 Germany
PAGES 18, 53

Komarow Design
214 Lincoln St.
Boston, MA 02134 U.S.A.
PAGE 132

Lambert Design Studio
7007 Twin Hills Avenue, Suite 213
Dallas, TX 75231 U.S.A.
PAGES 133, 159

The Leonhardt Group
1218 Third Avenue, #620
Seattle, WA 98101 U.S.A.
PAGES 120, 155, 174

The Letterbox
Suite One, 7th Floor,
289 Flinders Lane
Melbourne, VIC 3000 Australia
PAGE 96

Lewis Moberly
33 Greese Street
London W1P 2LP England
PAGES 42, 46, 66, 114

London Road Design
535 Ramona St., #33
Palo Alto, CA 94301 U.S.A.
PAGE 160

Lorenc Design
724 Longleaf Drive NE
Atlanta, GA 30342 U.S.A.
PAGES 24, 125, 168

Mark Oliver, Inc.
1 West Victoria Street
Santa Barbara, CA 93101 U.S.A.
PAGE 43

Mário Aurélio & Associados
R. Cidade Recife 232 3E
Oporto 4200 Oporto, Portugal
PAGES 47, 133, 136, 155

Matite Giovanotte
Via Degli Orgogliosi, 15
Forli, FO L7100 Italy
PAGES 50, 76

Melia Design Group
905 Bernina Ave.
Atlanta, GA 30307 U.S.A.
PAGES 54, 145, 162

Michael Schwab Design
80 Liberty Ship Way #7
Sausalito, CA 94965 U.S.A.
PAGE 108

Michele Rayome, Designer
5334 Westport Road, Apt. #8
Madison, WI 53704 U.S.A.
PAGE 166

Monnens-Addis Design
2515 Ninth St.
Berkeley, CA 94710 U.S.A.
PAGE 51

Nicholas Associates
213 W. Institute Place, #704
Chicago, IL 60610 U.S.A.
PAGES 23, 41, 89

Office B Pty Ltd
Level 7, 159 Kent Street
Sydney, NSW 2000 Australia
PAGE 171

The Office of Mayer + Myers
1148 South 7th Street
Philadelphia, PA 19147 U.S.A.
PAGE 73

Olaf Becker
Burg Eltz Weg 5
Munich 81375 Germany
PAGES 14, 70

Overdrive Design Ltd
37 Hanna Ave., Door 2, 2nd Floor
Toronto, ON M6K 1W9 Canada
PAGES 80, 94

Parham Santana
7 W. 18th St.
New York, NY 10011 U.S.A.
PAGE 151

Pea Pod Studio
3021 Linwood Ave.
Baltimore, MD 21234 U.S.A.
PAGE 58

Pentagram Design Ltd
11 Needham Road
London W11 2RP England
PAGES 3, 56, 136

Philip Fass
1310 State Street
Cedar Falls, IA 50613-4128 U.S.A.
PAGES 10, 71

The Pitcock Design Group
1011 Hickory Road
South Bend, IN 46615 U.S.A.
PAGES 119, 128

Platinum Design
14 W. 23rd
New York, NY 10010 U.S.A.
PAGES 146, 167

The Q Design Group
20 Birch Hill Road
Weston, CT 06883 U.S.A.
PAGE 78

Rauscher Design Inc.
1501 Story Ave.
Louisville, KY 40206 U.S.A.
PAGES 4, 54, 154

Resolute Communications Design
8106 Valley Drive
Palos Hills, IL 60465 U.S.A.
PAGE 139

Richard Endly Design, Inc.
510 First Ave. N., Suite 206
Minneapolis, MN 55403 U.S.A.
PAGE 92

Robin Shepherd Studios
476 Riverside Ave.
Jacksonville, FL 32202 U.S.A.
PAGES 110, 121

Sackett Design Associates
2103 Scott Street
San Francisco, CA 94115-2120
U.S.A.
PAGES 57, 62

Sayles Graphic Design
308 Eighth Street
Des Moines, IA 50309 U.S.A.
PAGES 30, 31 107, 108, 128

Seton Hall University
457 Centre Street
South Orange, NJ 07079 U.S.A.
PAGE 76

Sexton Design
63 Hallam Street
San Francisco, CA 94103-3906
U.S.A.
PAGES 153, 167

Sharisse Steber, c/o Supon Design Group
1700 K Street, NW, Suite 400
Washington, DC 20006 U.S.A.
PAGE 137

Sheehan Design
2505 Second Ave., #700
Seattle, WA 98121 U.S.A.
PAGES 52, 144

Sheirer Graphic Design
27 Linden St.
Frostburg, MD 21532 U.S.A.
PAGE 157

Shelby Designs & Illustrates
155 Filbert Street, #216
Oakland, CA 94607 U.S.A.
PAGE 157

Sineerat Panpumchuen
223 E. Jones Lane
Savannah, GA 31401 U.S.A.
PAGE 19

Spatchurst Design Associates
230 Crown Street
Darlinghurst, NSW 2010 Australia
PAGES 60, 169

Springer & Jacoby Werbung GmbH
Poststrasse 14-16
Hamburg 20354 Germany
PAGES 74

Supon Design Group
1700 K Street, NW, Suite 400
Washington, DC 20006 U.S.A.
PAGES 43, 155, 161, 164, 167

Studio M D
1512 Alaskan Way
Seattle, WA 98101 U.S.A.
PAGES 103, 104

Tayburn Ltd
15 Kittle Yards, Causewayside
Edinburgh EH9 1PJ Scotland
PAGE 43

The Team Design Consultants
120 Putney Bridge Road
London SW15 2NQ England
PAGE 59

Telmet Design Associates
398 Adelaide Street West
Toronto, ON M5V 1S7 Canada
PAGE 157

Thibault Paolini Design
19 Commercial Street
Portland, ME 04101 U.S.A.
PAGE 55

Three Communication Design
1807 W. Sunnyside, 2C
Chicago, IL 60640 U.S.A.
PAGE 142

Tim Girvin Design, Inc.
1601 2nd Ave., Fifth Floor
Seattle, WA 98101 U.S.A.
PAGES 99, 109